I0813203

Berenice

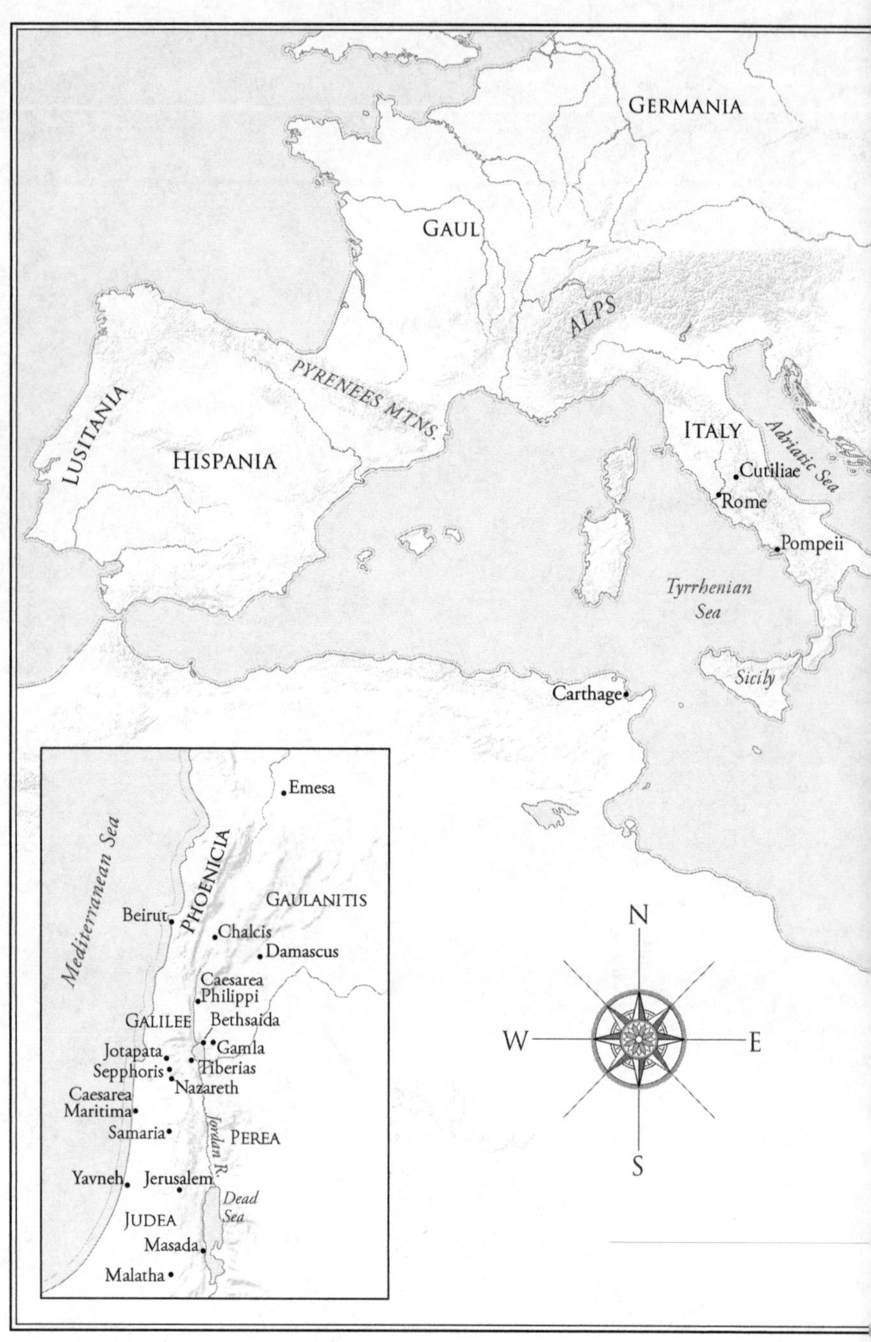
GERMANIA
GAUL
ALPS
PYRENEES MTNS.
LUSITANIA
HISPANIA
ITALY
Adriatic Sea
Cutiliae
Rome
Pompeii
Tyrrhenian Sea
Sicily
Carthage
Emesa
Mediterranean Sea
PHOENICIA
GAULANITIS
Beirut
Chalcis
Damascus
Caesarea Philippi
GALILEE
Bethsaida
Gamla
Jotapata
Tiberias
Sepphoris
Nazareth
Caesarea Maritima
Samaria
Jordan R.
PEREA
Yavneh
Jerusalem
Dead Sea
JUDEA
Masada
Malatha
N
W
E
S

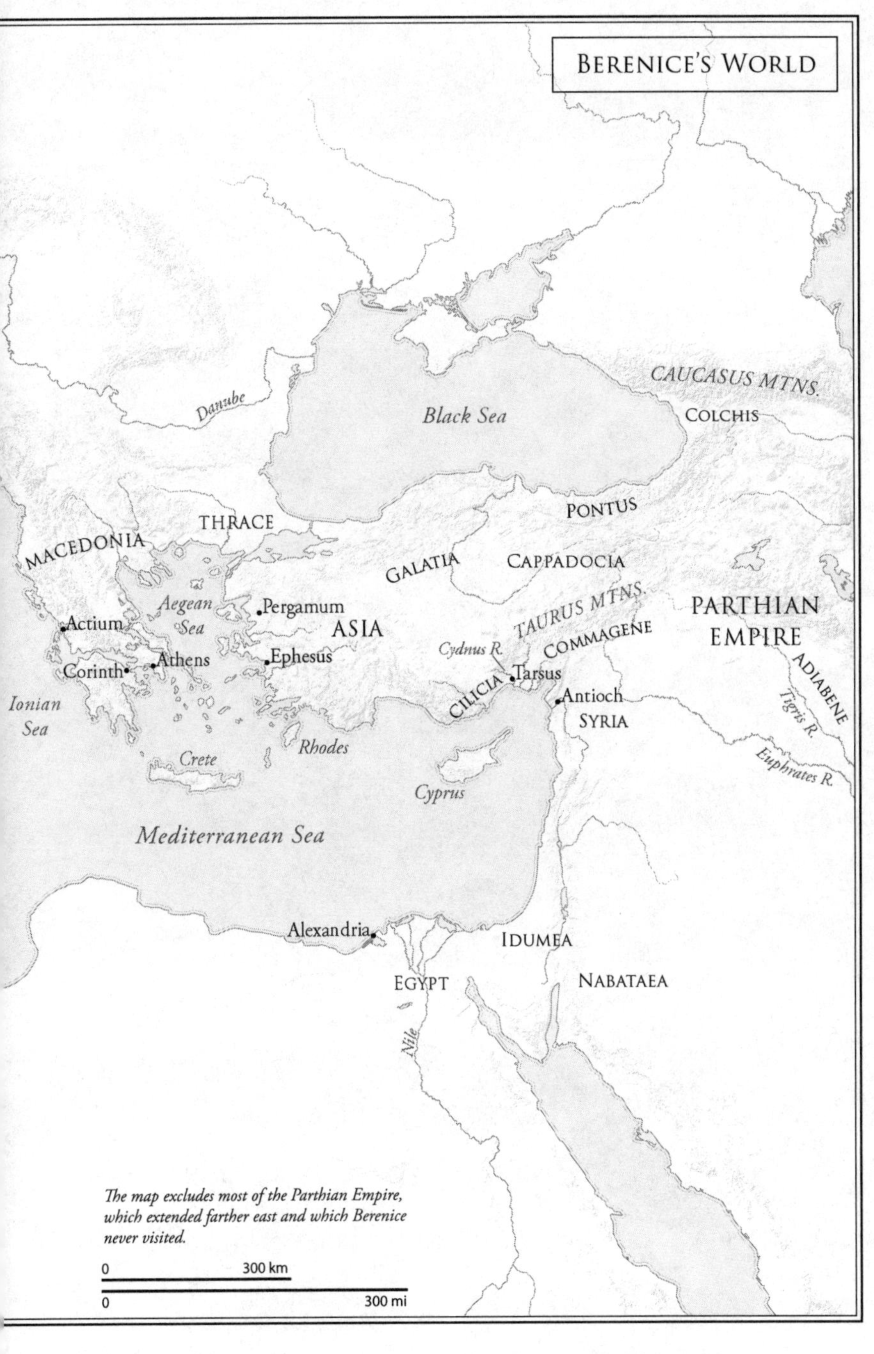

Berenice's World
Danube
Black Sea
Caucasus Mtns.
Colchis
Pontus
Thrace
Macedonia
Galatia
Cappadocia
Aegean Sea
Pergamum
Taurus Mtns.
Parthian Empire
Actium
Asia
Commagene
Cydnus R.
Athens
Ephesus
Corinth
Tarsus
Adiabene
Cilicia
Antioch
Ionian Sea
Tigris R.
Syria
Rhodes
Crete
Euphrates R.
Cyprus
Mediterranean Sea
Alexandria
Idumea
Egypt
Nabataea
Nile
The map excludes most of the Parthian Empire, which extended farther east and which Berenice never visited.
0
300 km
0
300 mi

Berenice

Queen in Roman Judea

Bruce Chilton

· ANCIENT LIVES ·

Yale
UNIVERSITY PRESS
NEW HAVEN & LONDON

Published with assistance from the Louis Stern Memorial Fund.

Yale University Press books may be purchased in quantity for educational, business, or promotional use. For information, please e-mail sales.press@yale.edu (U.S. office) or sales@yaleup.co.uk (U.K. office).

Frontispiece: Beehive Mapping.

Set in the Yale typeface designed by Matthew Carter, and Louize, designed by Matthieu Cortat, by Integrated Publishing Solutions.
Printed in the United States of America.

Library of Congress Control Number: 2025934833
ISBN 978-0-300-27425-7 (hardcover)

A catalogue record for this book is available from the British Library.

Authorized Representative in the EU: Easy Access System Europe, Mustamäe tee 50, 10621 Tallinn, Estonia, gpsr.requests@easproject.com.

10 9 8 7 6 5 4 3 2 1

· ANCIENT LIVES ·

Ancient Lives unfolds the stories of thinkers, writers, kings, queens, conquerors, and politicians from all parts of the ancient world. Readers will come to know these figures in fully human dimensions, complete with foibles and flaws, and will see that the issues they faced – political conflicts, constraints based in gender or race, tensions between the private and public self – have changed very little over the course of millennia.

James Romm
Series Editor

Contents

Introduction 1

PART I: BECOMING QUEEN

Chapter One. Child Bride in Alexandria 11

Chapter Two. Queen of Chalcis 29

PART II: ROMAN INFLUENCER

Chapter Three. Sister of Agrippa II 51

Chapter Four. Wife of King Polemon 67

PART III: IMPERIAL CONSORT

Chapter Five. Penitent in Jerusalem 91

Chapter Six. Titus's Paramour in Rome 109

Epilogue 129

Chronology 149

Genealogy 153

Source Notes 155

Notes 159

Bibliography 177

Acknowledgments 187

Index 189

Berenice

Introduction

The name Berenice expresses the ambition of the Herodian dynasty. In Greek, the elite language of the Roman Empire, the feminine form *Berenike* conveys the meaning "victory-bearer," and the name was used for centuries in Egyptian dynasties. Berenice's Judean parents, who conceived her during their quest for power, clearly named her for the desired result of their quest: the triumph of their family. And Berenice would live up to her parents' aspirations, identifying and mastering sources of power in the first century CE, first in the Roman province of Judea and its associated realms, and then across the Roman Empire as a whole. Throughout her lifetime she was proudly – and when occasion demanded, heroically – a practitioner of Judaism, although not the same Judaism that the religious authorities known as the rabbis established long after her death. Her insinuation into Roman imperial politics was so deep that she emerged as a key figure in the hectic events that resulted in the destruction of the Temple in Jerusalem under the general Titus in 70 CE. Once her attempts to protect the Temple had failed, she turned to protecting her family, herself, and the hope that the Temple might be restored. By the time an arch in the Forum was dedicated to Titus's victory a decade later, Berenice had taken up residence in Rome, had been his mistress for a dozen years, and was widely known by both supporters and detractors to be his consort; when Titus became emperor in 79, Berenice's status became an impediment to the acceptance of his rule and therefore an issue of state.

After the first century, Berenice was still remembered even in death, but no longer as the great-granddaughter of the best-known king of Roman Judea, Herod the Great, and the most prominent Herodian of her generation. Instead, her notoriety turned her into a punchline in the sixth satire of Juvenal, published early in the second century. Juvenal used Berenice's reputation to make his central argument that marriage should be avoided. He imagines the all too predictable abandonment of a husband by his wife, who takes valuables along with her, including a ring that once belonged to Berenice: "Big crystals are removed, as well as huge chunks of sapphire, along with a famous diamond, made more precious by Berenice's finger, which the barbarian Agrippa once gave for his incestuous sister to wear, where barefoot kings observe sabbaths as feasts, and custom grants clemency to elderly pigs."[1] Multiple marriages, rumors of incestuous relations with her brother (Agrippa II of the Herodian dynasty), and the last scandalous liaison of her life, with the Roman general and then emperor Titus: all these contributed to Berenice's celebrity as – in the words of nineteenth-century historian Theodor Mommsen – a "Cleopatra in miniature" (*Kleopatra im kleinen*).[2]

The territories of Berenice's governance were much smaller than Cleopatra's, and she lived more than a century later; moreover Titus had her depart from Rome rather than follow Antony's example of killing himself at the prospect of losing his paramour. Still, perhaps the only thing surprising about Mommsen's sobriquet is that it took so long for it to be coined. Juvenal does not mention Berenice's last known affair, a decision that avoided complicating his already fraught relationship with the imperial court. But Juvenal knew, and in any case it was widely known, that Berenice had been positioned by Titus so as to exert powerful influence and shape policies of state. Indeed, Berenice came to the brink of wielding imperial authority. At the close of the first century, the jurist Quintilian claimed that he personally argued cases before Berenice in Rome, as if she were somehow acting as a deputy for the emperor. A century and a quarter later the historian Dio Cassius complained that during this period in Rome she behaved "in every respect as if she were his wife."[3] This and other grievances against her during the second century and later, articulated postmortem, reveal an unease about how closely she had come to the center of power, and confirm an anxiety in regard to her deep and abiding cultural influence. Juvenal does not openly satirize Titus as he does Domitian, but he reveals his feelings about Titus's affair in his description of Berenice.

Part of what made Berenice an irresistible target for Juvenal was his strident anti-Semitism, a common prejudice during his time. His warning to the Romans to avoid countenancing Judaic practices seems positively Judeophobic: "Some with a father who revered the sabbath, worship nothing but the clouds, and the divinity of the heavens, and see no difference between eating swine's flesh, from which their father abstained, and that of man; before long they set aside the foreskin."[4] Berenice was perceived as a threat not only because she was a woman, but also because she was Jewish.

Berenice was also the sister (and more than the sister, if the rumor Juvenal perpetuates were to be believed) of a king, albeit a barbarian and barefoot king. Within the few lines of Juvenal's satirical character assassination, she is identified as bearing royal lineage, practicing Judaism, and – like her religion – threatening the Roman Empire from within. That threat was laced with sexuality in Juvenal's depiction, which perhaps made a comparison with Cleopatra inevitable, but what that later comparison misses is the anxiety that Berenice's Jewish influence caused in her own era.

Juvenal wrote from a safe distance in time after Berenice's death, and longer still after the death of Titus. During her own lifetime, public expressions about her could take a very different tone. In the Areopagus in Athens, a statue of Berenice was erected, probably in 63 CE; although the statue is long gone, its dedicatory inscription was published in the seventeenth century, giving her name in its Greek spelling: "The council of the Areopagus and the council of the 600 and the people for Julia Berenike, great queen, daughter of King Julius Agrippa, and a descendant of great kings and benefactors of the city – by the provision of the manager of the city Tiberius Claudius Theogenos of Paiania." The dating of the city manager, identified by means of a village near Athens, provides a relative chronology for the inscription, and his authorization of its wording attests to Berenice's status in his mind. Modern historians have suggested that Berenice is called "queen" owing to her association with her brother, or because she was the widow of a king who had died in 48. In fact the inscription mentions neither Berenice's brother (Agrippa II) nor any of her husbands, of which she had had three by the time the dedication was affixed.[5] Rather she is simply identified as a great queen, the daughter of Agrippa I in a long line of royal Herodian benefactors. Her contemporaries sometimes gave Berenice her due in a way that historians on the whole have not.

To assess Berenice in her time, and her influence within the various realms of the Roman Empire that both felt the consequences of her power and defined the environment in which she could act, this book traces her life as well as the contexts that she shaped and that in turn formed her. Each major phase of her development permits insight into how she was seen – and what ultimately she wished to achieve – over the course of a life that was more consequential than the considerable sum of its anecdotes.

Berenice's relentless involvement in the dynastic ambition of the Herodians left its mark in public acts. Some of them were designed for public consumption from the first; others were putatively private matters that became public, and were so controversial that it is fair to wonder whether anything like privacy had ever been her governing concern. But in regard to her intent, all inquiry unfolds under the disadvantage that there are no written sources in which Berenice herself comes to voice. She left no corpus of writing and, unlike her great-grandfather Herod, she had no Nicholas of Damascus to serve as her court biographer, propagandist, and advocate. What she had instead was a literary nemesis: the one-time Judean rebel turned Roman apologist known in most libraries as Flavius Josephus. In the last decade of the first century, he voiced the accusation against Berenice that her relations with her brother were incestuous, all the while portraying Titus in heroic terms and as a friend of Judaism. Josephus is not consistent in his portrayal; in an earlier work he depicted Berenice's courage during the mounting violence between Roman officers and Judean protesters that produced the revolt against Rome and then the destruction of the Temple. Only after Titus's death did Josephus discover his outrage in regard to Berenice.

The literary postures that Josephus assumes in his complex works represent a political program. Like Berenice, he was an actor in history, but his words exerted more influence than his deeds – and his words cannot always be trusted. Josephus's tendentious approach to narrating events and characterizing people has resulted in understandable reservations about using him as a source. In the case of Berenice, Josephus amounts to a factor no less distorting than Juvenal where sexuality is concerned. But awareness of how evidence is distorted cannot justify discounting what it says, since we have no independent access to Berenice. A biased contemporary is still a valuable witness, after correcting for the prejudices involved.

Indeed, those prejudices, expressed in relation to Berenice, are an index of how she influenced people in her time, favorably or not. People in history normally reach our attention through the medium of statements from them or about them in the past that reach the present. Those statements, close to or far from the actors at the time, always involve an assessment of the events in which they were involved. Even when a firsthand account by one of the actors is available, taking it at face value can scarcely be recommended. Rather, inquiry involves assessing the intent of a given action within its historical setting. Understanding events in this way enables inquirers to assess actions and contexts, whether or not the actors happen themselves to have produced part of the historical record. Obviously, private motives are not directly accessible during this process, but then assessments of that kind perhaps always lie beyond the ability of observers to articulate with confidence, especially many years after the event.

Berenice's intents might be gleaned from her actions, then, but they cannot be characterized in terms of her inner or emotional life. Her actions at key moments during the first century have evident motives, legible as a result of the contexts within which she acted, but her temperament is likely to elude definition, however refined our historical analysis might become. Whenever a single historical actor is implicated in several key events, however – as happens without question in the case of Berenice – then that person is embedded in those events, and her intents become increasingly plain as the differing contexts of actions elucidate one another. At such moments, the person has a *bios,* a life. A *bios* is not identical with biological existence. In the case of Berenice, in fact, her date of birth and her date of death are matters of inference. Her *bios* is instead a function of the meaning of her actions, from her own perspective, and from the perspective of those affected by her actions.

Even those in her time and after her time who sought to belittle or denigrate Berenice showed, by their vehement reactions, how she generated controversy and distress in the cultures within which she operated. Modern assessments of Berenice have also been clouded by anxiety and cognitive dissonance, because she persistently contradicts expectations of what it means to be simultaneously a Jewish queen and an influential Roman courtesan. Encountering Berenice, then, necessarily means not only learning about her life, but also questioning just what it means to engage in her history.

PART I

Becoming Queen

CHAPTER ONE

Child Bride in Alexandria

Berenice was born into a once-dominant Judean dynasty. By the time of her birth, several descendants from its days of glory had been vying with one another to restore Herodian power and influence in Judea, though her parents appeared to have been left stranded when Berenice took her first breath, around 28 CE. The political situation was in the process of radical change twelve years later as she took up residence in Alexandria, having been promised in marriage to Marcus Julius Alexander, a wealthy man of commerce, and the son of the alabarch of Alexandria, whose responsibility for the collection of customs made him powerful as well as rich. The title "alabarch," whose precise meaning remains uncertain, signaled prominence in the large Jewish community as well as the city as a whole. As part of his position involving the collection of Roman taxes, Marcus's father, named Alexander, had the opportunity to represent Roman interests on the ground as an administrator, and to curry mutually profitable relationships with prominent families in Rome and elsewhere in the empire.

Marcus Julius Alexander was a catch from a marital point of

view, and Alexandria was a major center of the culture of Judaism. The Greek translation of the Scriptures of Israel, called the Septuagint, was produced there, and the legend of its founding associates the Septuagint with the celebrated Library of the city. Alexandria is often described as the second city of the Roman Empire, after Rome itself, but culturally it was no runner-up. The emperor commonly called Caligula, whose schemes directly affected Berenice, her family, and all of Judaism, considered making Alexandria, not Rome, the center of his court as well as of his musical career.[1] Alexander the Great had founded the city, and its distinguished buildings included not just the Library, but also palaces, theaters, temples, and a huge and famous lighthouse; a perfect setting for Caligula's sense of his own worth.

The Jewish community in the city was of ancient standing and represented the confidence, diversity, and factionalism of diaspora Judaism. Among its elite, the brother of the alabarch, Philo of Alexandria, was a distinguished philosophical writer and theologian. In a sprawling commentary on the Pentateuch (the Five Books of Moses, or Torah), Philo made the case that Plato was the key to understanding Moses, and that Moses was the key to understanding Plato. When Plato spoke of ideal forms as the true basis of reality, for example, Philo claimed that Moses in the book of Exodus had anticipated him, because Moses's vision of how the Temple was to be built impressed on his mind a model of heavenly reality.[2] The Scriptures, throughout Philo's work, were to be read and commented on in their Greek version, and understood by way of analogy and allegory. He even referred to the position that circumcision was a symbol of obedience to God, introducing the idea that if obedience itself is present, the sign might be dispensed with. His consideration as a whole puts any such suggestion aside, but it is a mark of Philo's philosophical daring—and that of even more radical thinkers in the Alexandria of his time – that the implication is explored at all.[3] He and his relatives were in every sense leading figures in their occasionally fraught but always vibrant community.

Berenice, then, married into the most powerful and influential family in Jewish Alexandria. The Jewish community was only one of many in a city with many factions, frequent social turbulence, and egregious poverty alongside incalculable wealth. But she enjoyed a standing above that of any but the most privileged of Romans, whether Jewish or gentile. The path that had brought her to that status had been tortuous, and given her young age she clearly did not traverse it on her own. Her father, Agrippa, and mother, Cyprus, had carried her to this moment, and their sometimes harrowing journey had itself been possible due only to the unusual standing of the Herodian dynasty, both within the Roman Empire and within Judaism. Agrippa and Cyprus deployed those advantages in a meteoric achievement of power. Berenice at the early stage of her life was more a passenger than a driver in her parents' rise, but the contacts she helped them to forge in Alexandria also made her more than a pawn.

Berenice was descended from Herod the Great, who – with the sponsorship of Mark Antony and Octavian – had been declared king of Judea by the Senate in Rome in 40 BCE. Herod's father, Antipater, had already established the family as an effective supporter of both the Judean Maccabean state and the new Roman power, but it was Herod who became celebrated as *socius et amicus populi Romani* (an "ally and friend of the Roman people"), and gave his name to the dynasty. Augustus always held him in great regard, as he should have, given Herod's effectiveness as a warrior against Parthian incursions into Judea. Parthia's base of power lay far to the east, but fought successive wars with Rome in an extended conflict over hegemony in the region. After Herod accepted his diadem of kingship in Rome, years of battle alongside Roman forces were necessary to make Judea a secure state, and a bulwark for Rome against the Parthians. He effectively began his monarchy in 37 BCE, after a bloody but triumphant campaign as a general known for his military opportunism, his horsemanship, and his daring.

Herod's perils from within Judea itself proved more lethal during his reign than were the Parthians on his east. Among those who opposed his rule in Judea, some took to calling him a "half-Jew" on the grounds that the Maccabees had forced the practice of conversion on those living in Herod's native Idumea.[4] In fact, the accusation was spurious, since the Maccabean campaign during the second century BCE was conducted long before Herod's birth in 74 BCE. Although the charge still appears in some descriptions of Herod today, it should be put to rest. His Judaism and his family's were genuine, although they were not determined by the later expectations of Rabbinic Judaism, which arose during the second century CE and continues to define or at least influence current understandings of the religion in its many forms today. But it is an evasion to pretend to reconcile the discrepancy between Herod's religion and contemporary practice by turning him or his great-granddaughter into some sort of Jews *manqués*.

What did remain a problem for Herod within the realpolitik of his day was that he had no claim to monarchy, apart from his appointment in Rome and by Rome. For this reason, Martin Goodman's biography *Herod the Great: Jewish King in a Roman World,* might also have been subtitled "Roman King in a Jewish World." As Goodman remarks, Herod "had no inherited justification for his rule over Jews or anyone else."[5] But then not even the Maccabees could claim the legitimacy of Davidic descent; they traced their lineage as priests (and as such are known also as "Hasmoneans") by ancestry. Because the promise to the Davidic line in particular is articulated in the Bible (2 Samuel 7:4–17), alternative lineages such as those the Maccabees represented were always susceptible to challenge as a qualification for monarchy. The last known Davidic ruler named in the biblical books Zechariah and Haggai is Zerubbabel, who returned from Babylonia at the time of the Second Temple, by the close of the sixth century CE. Herod could not convincingly pass himself off as part of the Davidic line, but he did acquire royal status by association in 37 BCE by marrying a Maccabean princess named Mariamme. The aim was to connect his dynasty to the last great kingdom, before Pompey claimed Jerusalem and Judea for Rome in 63 BCE, to be ruled exclusively by Jewish rulers. The birth of two sons to Mariamme, Alexander and Aristobulus, seemed to assure dynastic success for this hybrid of Idumean and Hasmonean ancestry.

A combination of his family's unruliness and his own temperament, however, nearly undid Herod's plans. Despite his passion for Mariamme and her undoubted intelligence – or perhaps because of both – Herod became convinced that his wife plotted against him and had her executed in 29 BCE by strangulation.[6] He nonetheless saw to it that Alexander and Aristobulus were educated in Rome. By the time they returned to Judea in 17 BCE, jealousy among Herod's many surviving wives (totaling ten during the course of his life) and his numerous children had turned his court into a cauldron of conspiracy and rumor. Herod listened to the rumors, which were not entirely ill-founded, and slipped ever deeper into the conviction that his family wished to destroy him; he denounced his sons by Mariamme for conspiracy during an audience before Augustus himself. Augustus calmed his client king for a time, but then gave him leave to have the two young men executed; they also were strangled at Herod's order in 7 BCE. During the proceedings, the princeps was remembered to pun in Greek that one would be in a better position as Herod's pig (*hus*) than as Herod's son (*huios*).[7]

Those executions, toward the end of Herod's reign when he was dying from a type of progressive gangrene, went hand in hand with multiple changes in his will. After Herod's death and his spectacular interment, Augustus had to deal with competing claims among different sons, as well as with various wills and several wives. Through all that chaos, produced by Herod the Great's increasingly deranged behavior and punctuated by his slow, agonizing, and dreadful death, the emperor attempted to be faithful to the memory of his client king. He settled on dividing the territory of Herod's old reign regionally: Judea proper with Samaria, Galilee with a region on the east of the Jordan River called Perea, and Gaulanitis (which gives its name to today's Golan) above the Sea of Galilee, also with associated territories. Judea and Galilee were to be governed by Archelaus and Antipas, respectively – they were Herod's sons with their Samaritan mother, Malthake. Philip, the son of a woman named Cleopatra from Jerusalem, was to rule Gaulanitis. So it might have appeared that the Maccabean family line through Mariamme had come to the end of its prospects with the deaths of Alexander and Aristobulus. Events would contradict that expectation, but only because the politics of Rome as well as of Judea colluded to favor the prospects of Herod's project of a Idumean and Maccabean succession armed and backed by the force of Rome. The project that Herod himself had seemed to bury with the executions of Mariamme, Alexander, and Aristobulus proved resilient to a scarcely imaginable extent.

The family of Herod's dead son Aristobulus remained resourceful. Aristobulus's son was Agrippa, Berenice's father. He was educated in Rome, as Aristobulus himself had been, and showed from an early age two mutually reinforcing but not entirely compatible traits that characterized his actions: a gift for making powerful friends and a love of money and status. For most of his life, Agrippa urgently sought the friends required either to make wealth or, failing that, to create the appearance of wealth. He became close to Drusus, son of the emperor Tiberius and the imperial heir. That relationship enabled Agrippa to take out loans in order to finance a lifestyle that exceeded what he could fund on his own using proceeds from family lands back in Idumea to which he had access. Such a courtier's strategy was risky, since he was continually borrowing afresh to pay off debts, but it was possible to maintain because Drusus was so highly placed. Drusus died in 23 CE, so suddenly that it was widely rumored he had been poisoned. Agrippa, now exposed to the consequences of his own debts, and unable to repay them, sensibly left Rome. His only hope of remaining would have been if Tiberius had shown himself willing to protect his dead son's friend, but the emperor withdrew into one of the depressive isolations that periodically sapped his willingness to govern.

Agrippa retreated to Idumea, the ancestral Herodian land, to a place called Malatha; there he married a Herodian cousin named Cyprus. By the measure of children, their union thrived: Cyprus bore a son named Agrippa, commonly called Agrippa II as a convenience, and another – called Drusus after Agrippa I's deceased friend – who died before his maturity. That loss would prove increasingly consequential over time. Among Cyprus's daughters Berenice was the eldest, followed by her sisters Mariamme and Drusilla. In each of these cases, the children were both Herodian and Maccabean by descent. All the family lacked were resources and opportunity in order to make their royal nobility work for them. Agrippa I set about manufacturing the conditions to produce that result.

Had Agrippa I and his family lived and died in Malatha, they would scarcely be remembered now. But Agrippa I did not settle there, and he does not seem to have had any intention to do so. Antipas, the ruler of Galilee, was both his uncle and, since Antipas had married Agrippa I's sister Herodias, his brother-in-law. Indeed, the marriage of Antipas and Herodias was controversial, even by the standards of marriage with kin that client rulers of Rome favored, since Herodias had previously been married to Antipas's brother. This arrangement drew the criticism of John the Baptist, because it contradicted the Torah of Moses; Antipas then directed John the Baptist to be killed. The Gospels portray the execution as instigated by Herodias, while Josephus reports events without the famous dance by Herodias's daughter, who is not named in the Gospels. Josephus recounts Antipas's actions in terms of political expediency, although he does later mention a daughter of Herodias called Salome. That reference was woven together with the Gospels and later legends, reaching its most influential form in Oscar Wilde's *Salome.*[8] John the Baptist died as the result of a calculated political judgment with or without quasi-erotic machinations; whatever the circumstances of John's execution, after his death, Antipas with Herodias pursued a relentless campaign to advance his status and power. Part of that effort included founding a new city in honor of the emperor on the Sea of Galilee, named Tiberias. Four years after John the Baptist's death, that city would be Agrippa I's next stop in a bid to improve his fortunes.

Cyprus wrote to Agrippa I's sister Herodias from Malatha with a plea for help, on the grounds that Agrippa, in his isolation from power and influence, was depressed to the point of becoming suicidal. More than once, her interventions proved crucial to Agrippa I's rise, and her finesse was echoed in her daughter's ascension. In response to Cyprus's entreaty, Agrippa I was able to secure the lucrative position of market manager (*agoranomos*) in Tiberias, probably around 25 CE.[9] Since Berenice was born circa 28 (a calculation based on a later reference to her age in Josephus), Tiberias was probably the first place of which she was aware, and it was not a settled environment. Founded only in 19 CE by the ever-ambitious Antipas to honor the emperor Tiberius, the city as a whole became controversial when a cemetery was uncovered during its construction. This made the site unclean according to many Jews, and Josephus claims that Antipas had to provide subsidies to encourage people to live there, resorting when necessary to outright compulsion.

The dispute illustrates a vital factor in the Judaism of this period, known as Second Temple Judaism. As long as the Temple stood, it was the most prominent institution of Judaism, according to Scripture the single place on earth where the God of Israel accepted the sacrifices of his people. Whether practitioners came from Judea, Galilee, Egypt, Corinth, Rome, Damascus, or any number of other locations, their dedication to worship in the Temple made them Jews in their own minds and in the understanding of those around them. In English the two words "Jew" and "Judean" derive from a single Greek term, *Ioudaios* (*Ioudaeus* in Latin). For this reason, the ancient designation could signal belonging to a region, a people, a religion, or any combination of those. Knowing in which sense or senses the term was used in particular cases was and is a matter of interpretation, and arguments over what did or did not make someone a *Ioudaios* were perennial. Disagreements over what standards of purity needed to be kept in order to worship in the Temple were inevitable in that context.

The transnational Judaism of this period was enormously diverse in its practice, with the common standard set out in the Mishnah during the second century CE not yet widely agreed on. (The Mishnah, the compendium of the oral traditions of sages past and present, distilled the teaching of generations on how individuals and communities were to conduct themselves in light of the Torah of Moses.) The Talmud, too, a commentary on the Mishnah that became the classic reference for Rabbinic Judaism, would emerge only centuries after the Mishnah. Absent a common standard of teaching prior to the acceptance of the Mishnah and the Talmud, disagreements were inescapable, and the contention over Antipas's new city of Tiberias, whose governing purpose was to flatter the emperor, was typical of the volatile clashes that characterized Second Temple Judaism during much of its history. Berenice was exposed to the consequences of such disputes from an early age, without having any ability to understand them. Later in life, however, her behavior defined the commitments to Judaism that moved her, and before she reached her fortieth birthday, she would spell them out dramatically by means of her actions.

Berenice left Tiberias by the age of seven, which in antiquity was when a child became an actual person. Before then, her father's relationship with Antipas had deteriorated. Agrippa I was hungry for more prestige and more resources than the office of agoranomos could bring him, and Antipas was known to taunt him by calling attention to Agrippa's status as a poor relation. Agrippa saw the opportunity to move on by seeking the patronage of a longtime friend from his time in Rome, Lucius Pomponius Flaccus, who as the legate of Rome was the governor of the imperial province of Syria, based in Antioch, in which Judea and other dependencies were located. That important patronage also did not last long. By 33, the debt-ridden Agrippa had worn out his welcome in Antioch, denounced for accepting a bribe to influence his friend the legate. Flaccus in any case must have been ailing, since he soon died.[10]

During this period, Cyprus probably returned to Idumea with her children. Agrippa I had made remaining in Tiberias impossible for Cyprus; she was pregnant with Berenice's sister Mariamme, born in in 34, and at the same time was dealing with a young family and managing a vagrant husband. She also needed to finance the family with revenues from properties that were in Idumea; they demanded her close attention if they were to be sufficiently profitable to meet their needs in the reduced financial circumstances that Agrippa I's rupture with Antipas had produced. Meanwhile Agrippa himself traveled. Having failed in Galilee and Syria to restore his standing, he had decided to return to Rome, the heart of the empire, debtors on his heels.

The next few years were ones of remarkable changes of fortune for Agrippa I, and therefore for his family. He had staged his return to Rome by soliciting more funds, by means of a loan from Alexander, the wealthy alabarch of Alexandria.[11] Two connections facilitated that arrangement, and with it Agrippa's continuing access to resources. In Rome, Mark Antony's daughter Antonia with Octavia (the sister of Octavian) had been a great supporter of the Herodian family, since the time of Agrippa's mother, who was also named Berenice. Antonia was exactly the sort of Roman whom the alabarch aimed to please. She was the niece of Augustus, the sister-in-law of Tiberius, and the grandmother of Caligula, who succeeded Tiberius, and great-grandmother of Nero. Caligula gave her the title "Augusta," an honor confirmed after her death by her son Claudius when he became emperor. The power of her network was palpable, and of particular value to several members of the Herodian family. To distinguish her from an older sister, historians know her as "Antonia Minor," but that designation is hardly commensurate with her influence.

In addition, Cyprus convinced Alexander to help Agrippa, as she had earlier convinced Herodias and Antipas to do so. She made the journey to Alexandria for that purpose, and according to Josephus, she personally guaranteed the loan, five talents in its first installment.[12] Each talent was a bar of precious metal, amounting to some seventy pounds. On many occasions, Cyprus's behavior would prove to be influential on the still immature Berenice, as an example of service to her family, and in this case it may well have saved Agrippa I's life. To secure it required Cyprus's reputation as well as her wealth, to compensate for her husband's notoriety as an incorrigible and impoverished debtor. She disposed of her own wealth resourcefully in the support of her husband and her family, and Alexander the Alabarch took her word rather than Agrippa I's, and despite her husband's reputation.

In Rome, Agrippa found Tiberius with a new heir, his grandson Tiberius Gemellus. Concerned about the young man's welfare, Tiberius asked Agrippa I to travel with Gemellus; evidently, Agrippa I had lost nothing of his personal charm or of his allure as a man of the world. Agrippa was happy to help with Tiberius Gemellus, but he spent more time with the emperor's other heir-apparent, Gaius, the son of Tiberius's adopted son Germanicus. Gaius's vanity made him known in his own time and later as Caligula, "bootlet," after the miniature military gear his father Germanicus had given him during a campaign when he was a young boy. To Agrippa he was far more interesting than Tiberius Gemellus, because he was older and as dedicated to lavish banqueting as Agrippa himself was. Since Gaius's grandmother was Antonia, the two men were also natural allies through their connection with her. Understandable though their friendship was, it was most unwise for Agrippa to remark to Gaius in conversation while out riding in a chariot that it would be good if Tiberius would leave the scene so Gaius could rule, and it should have been fatal to say so within earshot of any servant.

Yet that is just what Josephus says happened, telling the story in a way that extends it and produces some inconsistencies.[13] Whatever the exact circumstances of Agrippa's comment, Tiberius was duly informed. The emperor of course needed to act, and he did act, despite Antonia's advocacy for her feckless protégé near the end of her life. Agrippa was not executed, but he was put in shackles.

Tiberius neared his seventy-eighth birthday, but he did not see it. He died near Capri in 37 CE, the same year as Antonia's death. Settling on the succession had become tortuous toward the end of his life, and Gaius managed to finesse Tiberius's will to his own benefit, succeeding his adoptive father and then eliminating the unfortunate Gemellus. At the same time he rewarded his friend Agrippa I. Three years earlier, Philip had died, and his territory in Gaulanitis and adjacent areas needed to be ruled on Rome's behalf. Tiberius, by this stage unpredictable in administration, had not replaced Philip, but ordered an interim administration, with revenues to be sequestered. Those revenues, and the whole territory with additions, were now all assigned by Caligula to Agrippa I, who was named as "king" of this land.[14] The friendship with Caligula, which had seemed his undoing, completely transformed Agrippa's standing, and his family's. The title of king, proudly flaunted by Herod the Great, had been denied to his sons; Archelaus had ruled as an ethnarch, Philip and Antipas as tetrarchs. Now his grandson, released from the detention Tiberius had ordered, restored royal standing to the family, albeit in relation to a peripheral fraction of the territory that Herod had once ruled.

In triumph, Berenice's father celebrated the remarkable status that his friend the emperor had bestowed on him. Agrippa I organized a grand procession for himself as he made his way from his lodgings in Rome to his new realm, with Alexandria serving as a crucial staging point in his celebration of newly acquired power.[15] The young Berenice had a special place in the proceedings, and her role was by no means merely ceremonial. Agrippa I arranged the marriage of his ten-year-old daughter to Marcus Julius Alexander, the son of Alexander the Alabarch.

Agrippa I had fitted out his royal attire before he left Rome; even his guards' armor was decorated with silver and gold, an observation made by Philo of Alexandria, the prominent philosopher who became Agrippa I's relative by marriage once Berenice was promised to Marcus Julius Alexander, since Philo was Marcus's uncle.[16] Perhaps that relationship explains why Philo describes Agrippa I as acting with modesty although his ostentation is patent, and why Philo credits providence with Agrippa's meteoric rise. Being close to Agrippa did nothing for Philo's objectivity. In fact Agrippa's opportunism, sometimes rash but certainly fearless and relentless, rather than anything like modesty, had resulted in his being the first Herodian since his grandfather, Herod the Great, to bear the title of king.

Still, Agrippa I needed yet more money in order to take up the role of a royal patron in his new realm. The marriage to the alabarch's son was strategic, and Berenice's age suggests that the need was pressing, though she would not be the only daughter whom Agrippa I contracted in marriage at a young age. The betrothal was not immediately consummated. Delay after the contractual agreement to a marriage was a matter of ordinary practice, but in this case more than that was involved. Agrippa I's immodest presence in Alexandria had provoked a riot; crowds of people whom Philo calls "Egyptians" paraded a homeless man in the city and addressed him in Aramaic as "Lord," as if he were Agrippa I.[17] Synagogues were burned and looted, and some were desecrated by mobs that set up a statue of the emperor in them. The situation was so serious that Philo went to Rome as part of a delegation to appeal to the emperor for relief. Agrippa I and his grand procession to and royal celebration in Alexandria had been spectacular, but not triumphant. The family took up residence in Philip's former capital, Caesarea Philippi, leaving Alexandria in chaos as they occupied the splendid palace that Philip had constructed for his residence.

Narratives constructed by historians of the time, Philo and Josephus (Philo's younger contemporary), relate the twists and turns of Agrippa's ascent with scant regard for Berenice. Her date of birth has to be surmised from a passing reference in Josephus; even her date of death can only be estimated. Both Philo and Josephus see divine providence behind the narrative of Agrippa I, but the man himself is to an exceptional degree the tool of that power. Josephus mentions, and only mentions, Cyprus and her daughter Berenice by way of relating Agrippa's move to Tiberias and his evident dependency on Alexander the Alabarch, which he secured by means of his wife's intervention and his daughter's marriage with Alexander's son. Because that is the case, Tal Ilan observed that during this period Berenice "was an object, acted upon by the real players in history, as most women (even royal women) in her time were."[18] At this and other points in her biographical monograph, Ilan is concerned to disencumber Berenice of her image as a little Cleopatra or some other incarnation of a sexual adventuress.

Without question, Berenice and her two sisters were all offered in marriage before or near the time that they reached puberty, a fact that marks them as sexual pawns in the great Herodian game. That is a vital consideration in assessing Berenice, at this and later stages in her life. Agrippa I, seconded by Cyprus, obviously contracted Berenice's marriage to Marcus Julius Alexander on their daughter's behalf, and so she was indeed an object. But they and several members of the family, including Berenice in due course, acted decisively on behalf of their dynasty by means of the marriages they contracted. Agrippa I's daughters represented political capital, and each of them proved to be part of a shrewd investment. The programmatic pattern is so clear that it would require some explanation to account for why the Herodian women themselves were unaware of it, or of their own important places in its execution.

When Agrippa I arrived in Caesarea Philippi, he struck coins that mentioned Cyprus, even as "Queen Cyprus," with her image.[19] Over time Berenice would occupy a cognate dynastic position, and then something more than that. Women such as Cyprus and her daughter Berenice undoubtedly functioned within their culture's paradigmatic expectations of their gender, and they may be surmised to have embraced those expectations, but their actions pointed to ambitions undaunted by conformism.

Those coins are also of interest because they intimate that Cyprus counted more in Agrippa's estimation than in that of Philo or Josephus. The steady denigration of the influence of women is an ancient phenomenon, more often than not exacerbated in the sources that reflect ancient events. Yet modern assessments have sometimes pushed that effect even further, by exaggerating what the sources say. One mode of exaggeration is to portray Marcus Julius Alexander as much older than Berenice. This represents marital arrangements that are already strange by modern standards as even more exploitative. The evidence suggests that Marcus Julius Alexander was an active businessman at the time of the marriage, but his age is not known. Further, Berenice was quite capable of divorcing a husband, a practice known among other Herodian women. Indeed, her great-grandaunt, Herod's sister Salome, had recourse to the expedient of having a husband killed after divorcing him.[20] Neither antipathy to the marriage on Berenice's part nor advanced age on her husband's part need be assumed. Another mode of exaggeration involves reducing the importance of the marriage: if Berenice's time before taking up residence is extended, that limits the duration of the union. From the perspective of the families, however, the betrothal signaled an enduring connection from the time it was contracted. Any delay in finalizing the marriage would have been due to custom, convenience, and pressing issues of the time – of which there was no shortage.

CHAPTER TWO

Queen of Chalcis

Berenice came to Alexandria to live with her husband, Marcus Julius Alexander, after 38 CE, when the betrothal was made. During this period, two of her new relations by marriage – Alexander the Alabarch, her father-in-law, and his brother Philo of Alexandria – were deeply engaged in fending off an unprecedented threat to the Temple in Jerusalem. Caligula gave the order that a statue to himself as Jupiter (or Zeus, as the god was known in Greek) was to be erected within the Sanctuary – a blatant violation of Judaism's prohibition of idolatry. Berenice's father, Agrippa I, proved to be a central player in dealing with the crisis, and his actions provided a precedent for Berenice's later intervention when the Temple was threatened again. Just as her mother's financial and diplomatic skills served her later, her father's capacity for drama became part of her character.

Owing to the centrality of the Temple within the practice of Judaism as it was then understood, the religion itself faced an existential crisis as a result of Caligula's threat. The actions of Agrippa I, in tandem with those of Philo, produced a stunning result, and it was one grounded in the good relations between Agrippa and the alabarch, of which Berenice was the personification. Her very name invoked a connection with Egypt and an allusion to its power; in practical terms, her marriage allied her family with the wealth and influence of a leading family in Alexandria that itself combined Roman and Judean interests. Agrippa I's spectacular new standing was grounded solidly in the interest that Antonia had taken in him, his status as an imperial favorite under Caligula, and his prospects as the first Herodian since Herod the Great to be named as a king. But an underlying factor was also Berenice's marriage into the alabarch's family, which helped transform Agrippa's financial position. She was not simply a victim of circumstance but also an agent of her dynasty's success.

Neither his luck nor his favor with the emperor had deserted Agrippa I, and his ascent continued once he had left Alexandria, despite the chaos he left behind there due to his actions. His uncle and brother-in-law Antipas, jealous that Agrippa had been accorded the title "king," made his way to Rome with his wife, Herodias, to ask that he be given the same status. Caligula did not react well, at least to some extent because Agrippa had sent him a letter that denounced Antipas as a plotter against Rome. Both Antipas and his wife were exiled to Gaul. Herodias refused Tiberius's offer to her, as Herod's granddaughter and Agrippa I's sister, to remain behind in Judea with income from properties. She preferred loyalty over ease, to Caligula's puzzlement.[1] But Caligula, in his own way, was also loyal, and he extended Agrippa's territory to include Antipas's former realm. As a result, the family was back in Tiberias, this time firmly in charge of that city along with Caesarea Philippi, and so instantly controlling both Galilee and Gaulanitis, formerly the realms of Antipas and Philip. Judea proper still eluded his grasp, but by this stage Agrippa I's intentions to accede to Herod the Great's full inheritance were plain, even if the circumstances needed to make the next stage of advance possible had not yet emerged.

Agrippa appreciated the importance of returning to Rome, both to acknowledge his gratitude to Caligula and to secure the public recognition there of his newly expanded realm as king. His decision to travel put him at exactly the right place and time to intervene in the crisis of Caligula's making. When the emperor came up with his impossibly provocative scheme of self-deification by means of Judaism's Temple, desperate means were needed to prevent the devastation that would have resulted from it. Events in Alexandria had not put the emperor off Agrippa; the new king's narcissism had provoked a riot, but the emperor, still young in office, was not a stranger to that fault himself. The various embassies that Caligula received from Jews who protested their treatment, and from the group Philo called "Egyptians" who objected to Jewish behavior, taxed his sometimes limited patience. He had heard of mobs who had set up statues of him in some Alexandria's synagogues, and the anti-Jewish apologist Apion pursued his line of argument by portraying Jews as the only denizens of the Roman Empire who were not willing to acknowledge the emperor's divine beneficence. The argument planted a sinister seed in Caligula's mind.

Gaius's attention by this stage of his life (still in his twenties, and fiercely making up for his subjugated status while Tiberius was alive) focused on the devotion that he believed he deserved. Apion's onslaught could claim support from a report that had come in from Yavneh, a town on the coastal plain west of Jerusalem, that a local mob had destroyed an altar that the gentiles of the city had erected in honor of the emperor.[2] Philo of Alexandria, by his own account an effective representative of Jews in Alexandria, contested Apion's charges, and by all the evidence he was a clearer thinker than Apion, and might well have been a more effective speaker. But he used no fewer words than his opponent, and Gaius lost patience with the back and forth arguments and at last cut off discussion. He even had Berenice's father-in-law Alexander the Alabarch, who was with Philo in Rome, thrown into prison.[3] Taken by Apion's accusation that the Jews denied him the divine honors he was due, Caligula devised his stratagem to resolve all disputes of the sort that had erupted in Alexandria. It appeared simple, direct, and straightforward. Confronted with verbose complexity, and religious disputes over his authority that in principle might break out anywhere in the Roman Empire, the emperor's narcissism had led to a bold solution.

Gaius ordered a new legate into Syria, named Petronius, to replace Vitellius – who had been Tiberius's man in any case. He commanded Petronius to take his forces into Jerusalem to execute his stratagem: set up a statue to the emperor as Jupiter within the Temple. The response to the threatened sacrilege, a public policy that was clearly announced, was instantaneous. Even the Roman historian Tacitus acknowledged that Gaius had made open war inevitable.[4] Petronius was met by thousands of protesters in his march to Jerusalem. The climax of the confrontation transpired at Tiberias, now the center of Agrippa I's realm, where thousands of people anticipated Petronius's arrival.

Demonstrations lasted over a month, while leaders of the city pleaded with Petronius not to act on the order he had received. Public opposition, they insisted, would be to the death, because the imperial order violated the recognition of the Temple and of Judean worship that had been honored since the time of the republic and fixed by the arrangement of Augustus with Herod the Great. Erecting the statue would bring on a revolution that would devastate and weaken the land as a bulwark against Parthia; the people would die rather than violate their laws, and their protest was already interfering with their tending to the land. Any failure of the crops would only mean distress, desperation, rising criminality, and violence aimed at Rome.

Petronius, at great personal risk, allowed himself to be persuaded, and wrote to Rome with a request that the order be rescinded. Meanwhile, King Agrippa I's presence in Rome, and his skill as a courtier, enabled him to discharge his greatest service to Judaism. Philo and Josephus agree in their evaluation of the king, although their narratives part company concerning Agrippa's specific actions.

According to Josephus, Agrippa I was an extraordinary host, and because Gaius regularly spent beyond his own considerable means, he appreciated the same trait in Agrippa. The king decided to put on a sumptuous feast beyond even the extravagance of the emperor's imperial fare, and of course Gaius was the guest of honor. Josephus depicts a well-fed and intoxicated emperor asking Agrippa for any favor he would like.[5] Agrippa took what he knew very well was a risk, and asked Gaius to abandon the order already given to Petronius.

Given Gaius's frame of mind, and his usual pride in refusing to rescind resolutions he had once made, Agrippa's courage was evident, just as his lack of self-concern in that moment was quite out of character. Gaius's reaction was even more startling. He replied that he would send another message to Petronius, commending him for the rapid deployment of his soldiers. Taking that preparation as fulfilling the original order, Gaius allowed that, if the statue had already been erected, it was to remain in the Temple, but that if it were not in place, the army might be dismissed, and the ordinary demands of governance taken up.

For all the doubts that have plagued Agrippa I's claim to practice Judaism (from his own time until the most recent historians), his courage in making his request to Caligula remains. The emperor's cruelty was legendary, his self-esteem famously fragile, and after all an imperial order had already been given. The request could easily have started what seemed like an impending bloodbath with the shedding of Agrippa's own blood. According to Josephus, Agrippa even decided not to ask for additional territory at the time, as he might have. If so, showing such reticence was good politics. Agrippa was aiming for the crown of Judea by this stage, and still he honed methods calculated to achieve that objective, although no immediate way forward in the circumstances that Caligula's order had created could yet be discerned.

Philo depicts the scene somewhat differently, claiming that Agrippa knew nothing of Gaius's edict, but noticed during an interview that the emperor was agitated. When Gaius explained his own anger and referred to his order, Agrippa fainted dead away when he heard what was planned. Only after his recovery in his Roman home could he beseech the emperor to rescind his order, which he did by letter rather than in person. Within Philo's narrative, fainting spells and other emotional crises abound when the proposed statue and the desecration of the Temple are brought up in Judean hearing. It is Philo's way of expressing the powerful reactions that Tacitus refers to. The alleged letter is a stately reflection of Philo's own theology, down to the Platonic definition of God as the maker and father of all.[6] The secondary literature has largely followed Josephus in his recitation of events at this time, although his lavish scene of banqueting echoes the biblical depiction of Esther's courage, in chapter 7 of the book named after her, and her effectiveness in the midst of extravagance. Yet Philo was very near the events described, while Josephus was far away and still a child at the time they unfolded.

How close Agrippa I had come to disaster was demonstrated when Petronius's message, which also asked Gaius to rescind the order, arrived in the imperial court after the conversation between the emperor and his client king. Gaius, enraged that a subordinate had questioned his command and reactive to any intimation that Judea might rise in revolt, wrote to Petronius again. He accused him of accepting bribes and directed him to take his own life, implicitly an offer to avoid a more grisly form of execution and the confiscation of any legacy that might remain for his heirs.[7] Petronius had by every appearance ruined his career and shortened his life, while Agrippa had just managed to prevail on the emperor's goodwill and his desire to appear benevolent toward a loyal friend, only to see his design threatened by Gaius's rage against the same request made by another man.

Both in Tiberias and in Rome, Agrippa's court had stood behind the nearly successful effort to change Roman policy. Yet Gaius's anger at Petronius spilled over into his high regard for Agrippa, and he began to make arrangements to restrict Agrippa's authority, so that the plan for the statue's installation could continue under Petronius's replacement. His order was now for the statue to be made in Rome, and then set up with a dedication to himself in Jerusalem as the "New Epiphany of Zeus."[8] By this stage, Gaius also planned a tour in order to take in Alexandria as part of a program of self-deification, and even to remain there.[9] In this way, he stirred within the Senate and even the imperial court the old Roman fears of Egyptian intrigue that had helped bring down Antony and his lover Cleopatra.

Although at the time of his accession Gaius was attractive to many people as a charming rogue, the sociopathic depths of his narcissism had become apparent to Rome's ruling class. The crisis exerted a profound influence at the time, and reverberated in literary sources for decades after the edict of Gaius. Within Jerusalem and throughout the Mediterranean world, Jewish opinion showed a new passion for the Temple, prompted by accounts of the episode of Gaius's arrogance (such as Philo's *Embassy to Gaius*). Gaius's endorsement of popular efforts to set up worship sites for himself and his family invited direct and sometimes violent Jewish resistance.[10] Some practitioners, including Philo, aligned themselves closely to the Herodians, and increasingly saw Agrippa I's role as providential, because he defended the Temple's integrity while avoiding violence.

A conspiracy, led by a tribune of the Praetorian Guard named Chaera, succeeded in cutting Gaius down as he made his way to observe the Palatine games in 41 CE. According to the Roman historian Suetonius, his corpse bore more than thirty wounds.[11] Caligula's death was hailed as providential at the time and long thereafter. By a combination of Petronius's daring, Chaera's fortitude, Philo's diplomacy, and Agrippa I's personal intervention, the tyrant had been stopped and the Temple had been saved. The assassination threw Roman politics into chaos, but the definitive annulment of Gaius's plans also produced a realignment in Roman policy toward Judea and Judaism, reprieved Petronius, and created a stunning opportunity for Agrippa by enhancing his prestige.

During this time, Agrippa's presence in Rome had been vital, and as a member of the Jewish embassy to Gaius, Philo of Alexandria had also played a role. The connection by marriage reinforced the religious connection that welded Philo, Agrippa, and Alexander the Alabarch to one another, just as it provided Agrippa with access to additional funds, as needed, from the alabarch. (When Agrippa engaged in gestures such as remitting property taxes in Jerusalem for a period, for example, considerable monetary resources were required, likely beyond the immediate range of even a royal income.)[12] The connection also served the posthumous interests of Antonia; those aligned with her stood to benefit from Caligula's assassination. Her son Claudius, who had known Agrippa since he was a child and shared a tutor with him, was now favored in the succession by the support of the Praetorian Guard. Agrippa also offered help in negotiations with the Senate, with the result that a grateful Claudius decided to reward this loyal courtier-king.

The extent of the reward was staggering. Agrippa saw his domains increase to include Judea and Samaria. These territories had been under the control of a Roman prefect since Augustus had removed Herod's son Archelaus from power in 6 CE. Archelaus had ruled not as king, but as ethnarch, and his brothers Antipas and Philip each controlled their own shares of territory as what was called a tetrarch. Pontius Pilate is the best known of the prefects; between 26 and 37 CE he had governed with a combination of shrewd calculation and brutish excess, of which the crucifixion of Jesus was just one example.

The arrangement of a prefect had been brought in reluctantly by Augustus, when it became clear that the son whom Herod had designated to rule, Archelaus, was simply too prone to massacring his own people and too inept to succeed. The story in Matthew's Gospel (2:1–18) of the Slaughter of the Innocents likely reflects his rule, rather than his father's. Although apologetic arguments have been deployed to defend the claim in Matthew's Gospel that Herod the Great was the ruler concerned, the chronology of Herod's death (4 BCE) and Jesus's birth (ca. 2 CE) challenges that view. Matthew's idiom in the passage is the typology of the Prophets of the Scripture in relation to Jesus, not historical narrative. The power of Christian legend made Herod the Great into an archvillain, and confused him with several of his sons. Fundamentalism has entrenched the inaccuracies, resulting in a badly skewed chronology and a historical misunderstanding of the differences among Herod the Great and his many successors. The repetitious use of names within the dynasty naturally leads to uncertainty, but the attempt to insist that the

New Testament is accurate, even when it obviously falls into confusion itself, is an exercise in self-deception.[13] The kind of violence reflected in the story, which is not targeted at known enemies but is vicious precisely in being indiscriminate, corresponds to the reason for which Augustus removed Archelaus from power in 6 CE. Now, however, Claudius made Agrippa I his grandfather's true inheritor in terms of both territory and title; what Herod the Great had made his own by conquest, and his son Archelaus had dissipated in his heedless acts of violence, his grandson Agrippa had acquired by dexterous diplomacy, intrigue, and audacity.

In Agrippa's resourceful campaign of acquiring royal power and restoring the fortunes of his family, Berenice had been a cog in a highly effective dynastic machine. Her marriage had provided Agrippa with the access to liquidity that he always required. Even when he became technically wealthy, from the time that Caligula had made him king of Gaulanitis, he required funds – for traveling with an increasingly impressive retinue, for providing his daughter with a dowry, and for showing the generosity expected of a powerful patron. Proceeds over time from royal buildings, which were tenanted, yielded an income that made their construction profitable, as Herod the Great had proven. But every time Agrippa advanced, adding Galilee with Perea to Gaulanitis and its surrounding territories, and later Judea and Samaria to the whole, additional immediate expenses needed to be met. At long last, his royal status had put him in a position to repay his debts without taking out loans to finance previous loans. He was still profligate, but no longer indulging his profligacy on a limited income. Wealth made all the difference in making the feckless princeling into an impressive king.

One of his acts in entering into his new realm demonstrated both his need for liquidity and his appreciation for Berenice. The core of Roman power within Judea was quartered not in Jerusalem, but in Caesarea Maritima. Once the prefect had lodged there, Agrippa I made the place his own. Because Judea lacked a natural harbor, Herod the Great had constructed an artificial one, dedicating the whole lavish project to Caesar. One of Herod's most impressive architectural projects, Caesarea Maritima combined Hellenistic elegance with the fierce practicality of exploiting the Mediterranean and its commerce, and of quartering the core of locally available Roman forces. In the manner of his new imperial protector, Claudius, Agrippa arranged for his palace to include statues of himself and his family. Among them was an image of Berenice, married although not yet a mother, and embodying the prospects for wealth as well as the ranging connections of Agrippa I's unlikely kingdom.[14]

The presence of Cyprus and Berenice in Alexandria had benefited Agrippa. His daring series of gambits – returning to Rome from Galilee and Syria just as Caligula was coming to power, securing funds for his triumphal progress to remarkable royal appointments in Caesarea Philippi and Tiberias, as well as going back to Rome for Caligula's final acts, the accession of Claudius, and his own inheritance of Herod the Great's entire kingdom – required connections in Alexandria. Cyprus's agreement with Alexander the Alabarch had provided access to liquidity for Agrippa, and Berenice's marriage to Marcus Julius Alexander sealed the newly minted king's relationship to one of the wealthiest families in Alexandria.

Agrippa's influence on Claudius was palpable in several imperial gestures. Claudius released Alexander the Alabarch from prison, and wrote a letter to the city of Alexandria that called for moderation on all sides. The emperor at the same time made a plea for the end of embassies such as those Alexander and his brother Philo had been part of.[15] Since Agrippa's ostentatious arrival in Alexandria prior to taking up his royal office in Gaulanitis had started all the recent trouble in the city, Claudius was in effect asking for the entire incident to be forgotten. The policy of demanding Jewish restraint was also reflected in Claudius's decision to restrict meetings of Jews in Rome itself. In particular, Roman Jews who believed in Jesus were singled out for removal, an adjustment that required expert advice for Claudius to make a distinction between one kind of Jew and another.[16] Agrippa was likely his adviser in that regard. As a favor to Agrippa, Claudius also named Agrippa's brother Herod (to be known as Herod of Chalcis) to be king of the region of Chalcis, north of Judea.

Dio Cassius reports that both Agrippa and his brother Herod gave welcoming speeches before the Senate, in Greek, to the new emperor. That is the exact event, in my opinion, that Agrippa celebrated by having coins struck to announce himself as "the great king," under his own name (without the prefix Herod), and as a way to swear his friendship to Caesar, the Senate, and the people of Rome. One coin shows both "King Agrippa" and his brother "King Herod" together holding wreaths over Claudius, who is styled "Augustus Caesar." Each king wears a diadem, yet is equipped as if for military readiness in cuirass over a subarmalis and tunic, while Claudius is in a toga and pours out a ritual libation.[17] Although designed to praise Agrippa I and Herod of Chalcis, these coins also represent Herodian fealty to imperial power and compliance with imperial symbolism.

Even as Agrippa pursued the politics of ingratiating himself to Claudius, he also pressed his influence over the conduct of the Temple. Herod the Great, his grandfather, had after all undertaken the mammoth task of renovation and extension that had made the site the largest enclosed space for sacrifice in the Roman world, and the central institution of what scholars today call Second Temple Judaism. In setting his sights on influencing the Temple and ingratiating himself by means of pious gestures, Agrippa revived Herod's project of asserting the family's combination of Idumean and Maccabean nobility, seeing to it that he, and consequently his children, would be accepted as royalty by Jewish opinion, not only in Roman law.

When Gaius released Agrippa I from his imprisonment, he had presented him with a golden chain equal in weight to the shackles that had bound him. After Agrippa passed through Alexandria, he traveled from his new base in Caesarea Philippi to the Temple and offered this lavish gift from the emperor there as an act of devotion.[18] It was a grand gesture, and his backing from the alabarch made it possible for him to appear with an impressive entourage. The performance was also deeply rooted in a sense of Roman history. Agrippa I had been named after Marcus Vipsanius Agrippa, the famed general, and then son-in-law, of Augustus. Herodians as a whole chose their children's names as expressions of a willingness to network within the Roman Empire and as statements of aspiration. Agrippa I stood in the Temple as the embodiment of Roman and Judean ambition, and he invoked legitimacy in terms of both realms.

Herod the Great had very wisely befriended the emperor's friend, and he had toured with Marcus Vipsanius Agrippa in various parts of the empire, both of them offering patronage as they went, with Herod traveling to be able to join the general who was, in effect, the second most powerful man in Rome. In his own territory, Herod named a city after Marcus Vipsanius Agrippa, and even inscribed his name on one of the gates in the Temple he was renovating.[19] Naming a grandson after him, none other than Agrippa I, came as a matter of course. The general himself showed visible affection for Herod the Great, and during a visit to that same Temple once arranged for the massive sacrifice of a hecatomb, a hundred oxen. Reciprocal gifting and lavish generosity were characteristic components within Rome's ruling class. As Jean-Michel Roddaz remarks, there can be no doubt but that prior to his death in 12 BCE the general Agrippa had curated connections among clients of the empire and with Herod in particular in such a way that the practice of Judaism, in Jerusalem and throughout Augustus's purview, directly benefited.[20] In the person of Marcus Vipsanius Agrippa, Rome approved worship in the Temple, with an implicit endorsement of its continuing sacrificial function. Agrippa I's golden chain, itself an emperor's gift, took up his namesake's gesture in a new idiom, since he was not a gentile, but was of priestly as well as Israelite descent. He represented the hybrid, imperial Judaism of which his own name had been an expression.

Just as Romans were capable of philo-Judaism without embracing the religion fully, so philo-Romanism thrived among many Jews, and not only in Jerusalem. In 47 BCE, Julius Caesar had been warmly acclaimed in Tarsus in Asia Minor, and people there came to call their city "Juliopolis."[21] Caesar's death in 44 BCE occasioned notable mourning among Jews in Rome.[22] It is not surprising that a later Jewish citizen of Tarsus, the apostle Paul, would call for obedience to the Roman rulers of his time in his Letter to the Romans (13:1–7). His argument articulated a conviction about the role of providence in governance that his younger contemporary Josephus would also come to take up. It is impossible to know in any given case whether endorsement of Roman hegemony was tactical or sincere, but a substantial sector of Jewish opinion incontrovertibly and openly supported Rome.[23] That support was generally more influential than the tendency to revolt, which also erupted on several occasions, most fatefully in Jerusalem during the 60s CE.

Agrippa I thoroughly understood the value of patronage. Once he became king of all Herod the Great's realm, he also took up control of appointing the high priest of the Temple, and magnificently provided for people to undertake a very public dedication known as the Nazirite vow, whose basic provisions are set out in Scripture, in the book of Numbers (6:1–21). Nazirites, male and female, would undertake to keep stringent purity for a period of usually a month, abstaining from grapes as well as wine, and avoiding contact with any human corpse. During the period of the vow they did not cut any of their hair, which was understood to become especially pure as a result of the process. Then they would shave their heads (and faces, as appropriate) and offer their hair together with animal offerings on the altar in the Sanctuary. Owing to the sacrifices involved, the whole procedure was expensive, and wealthy donors sometimes demonstrated their dedication to the Temple by underwriting the offerings of others to be Nazirites.

Agrippa I did just that, earning himself favor and setting an example for his children. Josephus is most concerned at this point in his narrative to emphasize the importance of the deposit of the golden chain, and he therefore mentions the Nazirite vow only fleetingly. But the Nazirite vow was more involved in terms of preparation and personnel than the histrionic gesture that Agrippa staged to assure his welcome into the Temple.[24] He pursued a deliberate campaign to ingratiate himself to those of his subjects most concerned with devotion to the Temple, by making himself a prominent patron of worship. By the first century of the Common Era, the Nazirite vow was internationally recognized within Judaism, and Agrippa's desire for recognition made him associate himself with it.

Following the policy of Claudius that he collaborated in shaping, Agrippa also had a follower of Jesus, James, the son of Zebedee, executed, as reported within the New Testament in Acts 12:1–3. This represented a calculated choice to punish an apocalyptic wing of the small movement centered on Jesus that from the Roman perspective could all too easily foment insurrection. The book of Acts adds a motivation for Agrippa by declaring that his action pleased the *Ioudaioi,* which here might be translated as "Judeans" or as "Jews." Either way, the remark is anachronistic. Most of Jesus's followers in Agrippa I's time came from Judea, and most were Jews; the term "Christian" became widely used only after his death, having originated outside the historic lands of Israel (Acts 11:26). Agrippa had James, the son of Zebedee, killed as part of his attachment to the Claudian policy that he had himself promoted: controlling the practice of Judaism by claiming adherence to its traditional forms, and assigning blame for any disturbances to minority movements within it.

Nonetheless, Agrippa I's high standing in the Temple did not sit easily, in the minds of many people, with his dedication to Roman practices and propaganda. While the Herodians on the whole had become masters at becoming all things to all people in order to rule as many of them as possible, to paraphrase Paul in 1 Corinthians 9:22, what seemed a necessary compromise to them could appear to others as a contradiction of Judaism, or even as hypocrisy. In fact, a teacher in Jerusalem named Simon publicly called attention to the conflict between the king's Judaic and Roman practices, and accused Agrippa of being unclean, and therefore not fit even to enter the Temple. Agrippa engaged in a public disputation with his accuser, and Josephus portrays him as winning the debate and generously bestowing a gift on the learned complainant.[25] But the tensions between Roman hegemony and the sacred authority of the Temple were not easily negotiated; nor were words alone sufficient to relieve them.

Agrippa I also had powerful religious supporters; over time the priest Josephus, born in 37 CE, would join in burnishing his memory. Still, Agrippa himself felt the need to use theatrics to solidify his standing and public acceptance in the Temple. According to the Mishnah, the founding document of Rabbinic Judaism from the second century CE, he staged a highly effective demonstration of humility. In his role as king, according to Mishnah tractate Sotah 7:8, he once read from the Torah in the Temple, and began to weep when he came to Deuteronomy 17:15, which reads, "You shall not place a foreigner over you." As he did so, those present are portrayed as shouting out, "Fear not, Agrippa: you are our brother, you are our brother, you are our brother!" For those viewing the spectacle with historical awareness, Agrippa I had brought the promise of his namesake, Marcus Vipsanius Agrippa, to its culminating fruition: the Temple was substantially and visibly under Roman protection. The scene represents a fond memory, written after the Temple's destruction and recollecting a time when the Romans not only endorsed the Temple's operation, but also let a Jewish king see to its welfare. Reminiscences such as Josephus's from shortly after the Romans burned down that same Temple in 70 and the Mishnah's from a century later need to be corrected for the effects of propaganda as well as nostalgia.

The point of the propaganda was to promote an ideal that all Agrippa I's family shared: control of Judea, as centered on the Temple, by means of the Herodian hybrid of royal status from the Romans and priestly status from the Maccabees. Agrippa had, by the very fact of his rule over Judea, achieved Herod the Great's aspiration for his dynasty when he married Mariamme. For continued success, the matter of progeny also had to be addressed. When Agrippa erected a statue for Berenice in Caesarea Maritima, he did the same for his younger daughter, Mariamme, and perhaps little Drusilla as well.[26] These daughters were crucial not merely as representatives of the dynasty, but as potential bearers of Agrippa's lineage.

The daughters' potential role in this regard emerged as vital to the survival of Agrippa I's wing of the dynasty. Agrippa's son was brought up in Rome while Agrippa I himself ruled. The son became known as Agrippa II, thus calling attention to his place in the dynasty, but he is never associated with a wife, and did not father any known children. Explanations for Agrippa II's apparent lack of a sexual history have flourished. One of them involves making him Berenice's lover from the time after he returned from Rome, although the absence of any children from this allegedly decades-long affair would then be puzzling. Such observations did not disturb Juvenal, and some modern historians have followed his lead in putting Berenice into an incestuous relationship with her brother. Then again, Agrippa II has been depicted as a homosexual with an aversion to "any physical contact with females."[27] Although homosexual practices in the Roman imperial court, with which Agrippa II had regular contact, are well established historically, the quasi-clinical finding that he could not bear to touch or be touched by women is of course beyond the competence of any historian to determine. Explanations of incest with Berenice and an unusual psychosexual adjustment operate well outside the limits of any historical finding.

Both sorts of explanation exemplify why Robin Collingwood, a distinguished philosopher of history as well as an archaeologist of Roman Britain, criticized the entire genre of biography. He disparaged biographers' interest in what he called the "gossip-value" of their subjects. Whether the aim is malice or sympathy, he argued, the biographer is after the emotional resonance of a person in history, while the historian is concerned with the rational thought expressed in actions, since, as he put it, "All history is the history of thought." Even Collingwood's followers have regarded his criticism of biographies as too sweeping, although the appeal of biography can indeed be limited to what he elsewhere called "cattishness," a species of voyeurism.[28] That is, biography can be an exercise in the reduction of a *bios,* a life, to its limitations: the conditions of biology, environment, and social setting that inevitably mark any life as a finite wrinkle in a fabric of functionally infinite scope. But in historical terms, a *bios* may appear in quite a different way. Instead of an object reducible to conditions, a *bios* may emerge as a subject that influences surrounding circumstances, and other human agents, in order to affect patterns of events and their meanings.

In the case of Agrippa II, the facts that he neither married nor fathered children are as much biological as they are historical. What remains plausible, however, is that by the time that he came to adolescence, whatever the causes and circumstances of his unknowable bio-history, his family was aware that depending on him for progeny could bring disappointment. Personal contact, information from intimate slaves, and observations of his social behavior would have come as a matter of course to his parents and his siblings. They were in a position to enable him to reign despite not producing an heir, a function that his sisters would prove to have no difficulty in performing. That, indeed, was a simple continuation of Agrippa I's consistent policy, of using the full range of Herodian sexual capital, and the family as a whole became party to it, in creating a means of succession. While they must have known or believed they knew why Agrippa II never married or fathered children, they are never recorded as referring to that knowledge.

Berenice proved pivotal in the dynastic quest for progeny. For reasons that are unknown, her husband, Marcus Julius Alexander, died when she was only fifteen or sixteen years old. His death appears to have been relatively sudden, because ostraca documenting his commercial transactions have been found dating to as late as the year of his death in 44 CE.[29] That same year, Agrippa arranged for Berenice to be married again, and his choice of husband was fateful. His brother and now king of Chalcis, Herod, had been widowed, and Agrippa contracted his daughter to him in marriage.[30] She was a contemporary of this Herod's son Aristobulus from a previous marriage. Whatever incongruities might have been felt, there could be no question that the Herodian lineage would be continued and from both sides of the marriage, provided only that Berenice conceived, as she had not with Marcus Julius Alexander. Once married to Herod of Chalcis, she was a queen. As a Herodian, however, her principal imperative was to become a mother: the iron requirement of progeny needed to be met.

PART II

Roman Influencer

CHAPTER THREE

Sister of Agrippa II

Agrippa I had advanced the Herodian agenda, which was indistinguishable from his personal agenda, with supreme assurance and surprising success. In addition to his consolidating his influence over the Temple and integrating himself within the imperial structure of power, his effectiveness on the ground in Judea was stunning. Working with the legate Petronius, his ally from the days of Caligula, he saw to it that a statue of Claudius was removed from a synagogue in Phoenicia, bordering his own territory, and placed where it belonged, in an imperial temple.[1] His effectiveness in that regard showed that his influence extended outside his own realm – as did his patronage, which resulted in a huge building project he organized in Beirut. Wealth and personal contacts were deployed together with political power, family prestige, and the widespread recognition of Agrippa I's imperial favor. The Herodian dynasty reached a status comparable to that enjoyed by Herod the Great, with Agrippa I achieving by political means what had come to his grandfather as a matter of military conquest.

When Petronius was replaced by Marsus, the new Syrian legate proved less cooperative; Marsus's fraught relationship with Agrippa may indicate that Agrippa's success sometimes aroused jealousy. Marsus reported back to Claudius that by reinforcing the defenses of Jerusalem, Agrippa had prepared the way for rebellion.[2] That cannot have been Agrippa's intent, since he was nothing if not loyal to Claudius, but the fact is that over the next few decades, the city of Jerusalem grew as a threat to Roman hegemony as a result of its increasing sense of autonomy, and as factional groups resorted to force, intimidation, and improved infrastructure. In particular, because the improved defensive posture of the city encouraged the resort to violent means, Marsus's complaint seems astute, and it quickly put a stop to the building in Jerusalem. But Agrippa found ways to work around the legate with lavish construction projects outside Jerusalem, especially the dazzling amphitheater, baths, and porticos in Beirut, where Agrippa also – in a characteristically Roman act of extravagance – hosted gladiatorial war games among prisoners that resulted in the death of fourteen hundred men.

When Agrippa I convened a meeting of client kings in Tiberias, however, Marsus objected again. Each man seemed to be jockeying for a more influential position than the other within the still plastic imperial system. Agrippa reacted to Marsus's dissolution of his attempted summit by arranging for a splendid celebration of games in honor of Caesar in Caesarea Maritima. Not even Marsus could object to this resumption of a practice that Herod the Great had instituted.[3] Agrippa's appearance at the event is described as spectacular both by Josephus and in the book of Acts 12:20–22. He appeared once more to be on the brink of extending his power, and as queen of Chalcis, Berenice helped reinforce the prospects of his legacy.

In Josephus's account, what happened next was tragic, a fated descent into ill health that led Agrippa I to die of a gangrenous condition eerily like that which had killed his grandfather, although his grandfather's descent into death was far more prolonged.[4] The rapid decline is, in contrast, celebrated in the account of Acts, since Agrippa had been responsible for the execution of James, the son of Zebedee, and for Peter's imprisonment. In Acts, Agrippa, who is repeatedly and inaccurately called "Herod" throughout chapter 12, is laconically described as eaten by worms, a feature that connects with Josephus's much more lavish description of the ruinous state of the maggot-eaten Herod the Great by the end of his life.[5] Whether lamented or celebrated, Agrippa's death at the age of fifty-four was unexpected. His family was blindsided both by the sudden loss and by the events that occurred in the wake of his death.

In Caesarea Maritima itself, the site of Agrippa I's recent triumph of self-promotion, some soldiers removed the statues of Agrippa's daughters from their pedestals and set them up over a local brothel. There the effigies were used in simulated sexual acts, so that the young but already twice-married Berenice was ridiculed as no better than a prostitute.[6] Any animus that Marsus held against Agrippa and his family was evidently felt more widely in the Roman ranks. Agrippa I's death unleashed forces of brutal, jealous aggression that had been contained but not extinguished during his life.

In his description of these events, Josephus refers to Berenice as being sixteen years old, Mariamme ten, and Drusilla six. That incidental reference is the fulcrum of a chronology of their lives. A much later source, the ninth-century *Bibliotheke* of Photius, relates Josephus's account of the pantomime sexual activity with an even more salacious edge, so that Agrippa's daughters are in effect portrayed as having been raped. One recent historian has been tempted to consider that really was the case, but the exaggeration seems as evident as Photius's dependence on Josephus.[7] Since his work is in the nature of a digest, composed with secretarial help, unless there are indications to the contrary it appears unlikely that it is a correction of the sources it cites as if it were based on superior evidence. Nonetheless, the insult was public and profound, and it was staged in the setting of violence that broke out in Judea and Samaria, while in Perea on the other side of the Jordan River local Jewish militants threatened full-scale warfare with neighboring Philadelphia.[8]

Claudius had straightforward access whenever he liked to Agrippa I's son, because the young Agrippa II was living in Rome. Josephus claims that Claudius considered naming him as his father's successor, although at the time he was only seventeen years old.[9] Given the long delay in Agrippa II assuming power anywhere, however, any such consideration must have been very brief indeed. Josephus's portrait of Claudius's hesitation in coming to the conclusion that he could not replace one Herodian Agrippa with another is clearly an example of Josephus's generosity in his portraits of Agrippa II as well as of Agrippa I. In any event – and probably without hesitation – Claudius dealt with the outbreaks of violence sensibly, by appointing a procurator, an administrative officer of the sort that Augustus had installed for Judea and Samaria when Herod the Great's son Archelaus had proven incapable of meeting the violent conditions of that period.

While Augustus had sent prefects to deal with the chaos of that time, the office of procurator carried more military and financial authority, just what Claudius now needed to see applied to the situation on the ground. Herod the Great's death had once spawned a series of revolts and attempted coups, which Archelaus had not been able to address; instead in the end he aggravated the problem with indiscriminate retaliation. That Claudius reverted to direct rule, and named a procurator rather than a prefect to the office, signaled concern in Rome in regard to the stability of Judea and Samaria in the wake of Agrippa I's death.

However understandable it might have been for Claudius not to turn to Agrippa II at this point, it represented a palpable setback for Herodian rule, one made all the more painful because the dynasty's territorial reach had only recently, under Agrippa I, been restored to its former extent. Having now lost Judea and Samaria, the most prestigious and powerful territories of their realm, and with the young heir still in Rome, Agrippa I's family would need to act with the dead monarch's kind of resourcefulness in order to redress their sudden and debilitating loss. On the ground and nearest to Judea and Samaria, Agrippa I's brother Herod of Chalcis and Agrippa II's sister Berenice would shortly supply the hope for restoring their family's fortunes.

Herod king of Chalcis and Queen Berenice were by default the most influential people in the Herodian dynasty. Herod, over fifty years old, was deeply experienced, fluent with the ways of the court of Claudius, and personally known in Rome. The twice-married Berenice was still a teenager, but she became a partner with her husband in recovering from the loss of Agrippa I, and from the overall reduction of Herodian territory that came with his death. Two ways forward were available to them. The first was the use of the Temple as a center of influence, prestige, and power, even while a Roman procurator governed Judea and Samaria. The second was the provision of a plausible line of succession for Agrippa I's family, with Agrippa II still unmarried and in Rome. In regard to the first, Temple-focused, strategy, Berenice provided an extremely useful connection at a crucial moment. In regard to the second, succession, Berenice was indispensable, since her sisters were as yet unmarried.

The procurator whom Claudius appointed in 44 CE, Cuspius Fadus, dealt vigorously with the unrest that had broken out at the time of Agrippa I's death. The most famous campaign was against Theudas, a prophetic revolutionary who gathered followers at the

River Jordan with the promise that, as in the case of the biblical Joshua, the waters would part for them and they would all cross into and inherit the land of promise. Fadus's squadron of soldiers ended their quest, and the decapitated head of Theudas was put on display in Jerusalem. The book of Acts mentions Theudas by name, although out of chronological order, while Josephus provides a brief but vivid description of the episode.[10]

While naming Cuspius Fadus as procurator, Claudius had removed Marsus, with whom Agrippa I had had such a contentious relationship, as legate. But the status quo under Agrippa I was not honored in a crucial matter; Cuspius Fadus decided, as a security measure, to keep the vestments of the high priest under guard—and under Roman control—adjacent to the Temple in the Antonia Fortress. The arrangement enabled the procurator to interfere with the timing of sacrificial actions that were the raison d'être of the high priesthood, since he controlled any release of the vestments. But the decision sparked protest, which ultimately played to the advantage of Herod of Chalcis and Berenice: after Claudius received envoys who traveled to Rome to complain, supported by Agrippa II, he reversed Fadus's decision. Josephus claims, by means of an eloquent letter that he quotes, that Claudius cited his own desire to promote the traditional religion of every land, as well as his friendship with Agrippa II and his high regard for Herod of Chalcis and his son (from a previous wife), Aristobulus.[11] Even in his death, Agrippa I had made Marsus and Fadus pay for their attempts to curtail his influence. The question for the Herodians was how to revive that influence under dynastic successors; in this their projection of influence over the administration of the Temple was a notable step forward.

The Temple was the dominant institution of Judaism, and at the same time a point of neuralgic concern for the Roman Empire.

Understanding its unique value to them both is vital to appreciating many events of the first century, as well as the motivations of Herod of Chalcis and Berenice. The Temple was Herod the Great's most enduring project. The great stone platform on which the Dome of the Rock and the Al-Aqsa Mosque stand today is a remnant of his enormous endeavor, which greatly extended the size and aspect of the whole edifice. The result served the elder Herod's purposes perfectly, both as a Roman king and as a Jewish ruler.

The Romans had been involved with one Jewish ruler or another since the second century BCE, when Rome and Jerusalem signed a treaty of mutual assistance quoted in 1 Maccabees (8:17–30), a work in the Apocrypha. At the time, Rome was still a republic and Jerusalem was governed by a priestly head of state under the Maccabees. As a result, Rome recognized what it called "the religion of the Jews" as a legal religion, even after Pompey marched into Jerusalem in 63 BCE and established Roman jurisdiction. Because Judaism refused idolatry, that recognition implied that Jews had the right not to engage in devotion to Greco-Roman gods, including the offering of divine honors to the emperor when that practice emerged during the principate. In a deft arrangement that gave the appearance of honoring the religion of the Jews while at the same time securing recognition of Rome's hegemony, the emperor provided for sacrifices to be offered in his name every day in Jerusalem. In effect, the emperor was not prayed to by his Jewish subjects, but they did pray for him to their God.

The autonomy of the Temple was deliberately circumscribed by the combined force of the treaty with Rome and Pompey's conquest, which assured Roman political dominance in the historic lands of Israel. Jewish subjects, however, were able to live throughout the Roman Empire, to practice their religion, and in some cases – most conspicuously the Herodians as a privileged family – to enjoy the benefits of citizenship. The agreement proved durable until the year 66 CE, and yet the issue of custody of high priestly vestments had proven sensitive. Earlier, Pontius Pilate, following precedent, had kept them in the Antonia Fortress, in order to assure himself that security was in place for the celebration of festivals before he released them. Pilate, best known as Jesus's executioner, was a cruel but effective prefect, who served longer than most in Judea. In the first phase of his tenure (26–31 CE), his actions were deliberately provocative. Most notably he introduced idolatrous objects – shields with Caesar's emblem – into Jerusalem and confiscated Temple funds in order to build an aqueduct.[12] After the execution of Sejanus in Rome in 31, however, Pilate had to adjust to the loss of his sponsor, who had been prefect of the Praetorian Guard. Adjust Pilate did, by making common cause with Caiaphas, the high priest of the time. In executing Jesus in 32, Pilate ingratiated himself to Caiaphas and, as written in the Gospel according to Luke (23:1–12), even mended his fences with Antipas after his interventions in the Temple. He did not, however, moderate his cruel behavior in regard to Samaritans, and that resulted in his exile in 37.[13] At the same time, the Syrian legate Vitellius restored custody of the high priestly vestments to the high priest. When Pilate was removed from power, custody of the vestments reverted to the priests themselves. This was the precedent that Claudius cited when confronted with the appeal against the decision of Cuspius Fadus.

Agrippa II had proven effective in convincing Claudius in Rome to overrule Cuspius Fadus. Herod of Chalcis took the opportunity, although he had no appointment in Jerusalem, to petition for authority over the Temple, the sacred implements, and the selection of high priests.[14] His wish was granted, so that hereditary control of the Temple could be passed among Herodians quite apart from the question of whether they could exercise monarchy over Judea and

Samaria. The arrangement was a major step forward for Agrippa I's wing of the dynasty. Herod of Chalcis lost no time in appointing a new high priest, which both solidified his power and signaled a possible advance in his own accession to Agrippa I's position.

Influence over the Temple had passed to the Herodians at the cost of the standing of Cuspius Fadus, and his tenure extended only until 46. The appointment of that year put Herod of Chalcis and his wife Berenice in a position to exert some influence on the regular governance of Agrippa I's former territory as well as that of the Temple. The new procurator was Tiberius Julius Alexander, whose name might seem familiar because his brother, Marcus Julius Alexander, had been Berenice's first husband.

From a prominent Jewish family, Tiberius Julius Alexander, as described by Josephus, was less pious than his father the alabarch, and for that reason some historians have described him as an apostate. That characterization is not well founded, although later we will see that during the war against Rome, his Roman loyalties superseded his Jewish sensibilities.[15] In that regard, however, he appears no more pliant than many other Jewish leaders of the period. Even Josephus admits that while in office as procurator, Tiberius honored Judaic custom.[16] Further, he supported Herod of Chalcis's authority over the appointment of the high priest, while seeing to the execution of sons of Judas the Galilean, a revolutionary leader who had protested the Roman census decades earlier under Quirinius. All in all, he managed a degree of relative balance and stability in the midst of famine, no small achievement.[17] The later trajectory of Tiberius Julius Alexander's career suggests that his replacement in 48 was not a sign of imperial displeasure. Yet that year brought another blow to the Herodians' hope for the restoration of their former glory.

Coordinating the work of the procurator with that of Herod of

Chalcis, a connection that Berenice's first marriage facilitated, had produced good results under difficult circumstances. While Herod of Chalcis had deftly pressed the case for his role in administering the Temple, and although Claudius had singled him out for praise, according to Josephus, when the emperor overruled Fadus, there does not seem to have been any serious consideration given to naming Herod of Chalcis to Agrippa I's former role.[18] Perhaps Claudius, while appreciative of Herod, preferred to look for dynastic succession among direct descendants of Agrippa I. In addition, at the time of Agrippa's death, and before his demise was widely known, his brother had acted swiftly to execute one of the family's most annoying, vocal, and prominent critics, an act that might have been seen as presumptuous in Rome.[19] Or again, perhaps it was known that Herod of Chalcis was unwell. Whatever was known about his health then is, unfortunately, not known now. Unexpectedly or not, Agrippa I's brother in fact died in 48, so there could be no question of his moving on from Chalcis to inherit more of the formerly Herodian lands. As in the case of Agrippa I, this death disrupted the success that the Herodian dynasty had positioned itself to enjoy. The most recent progress had not been as great as in the case of Agrippa I, but when Herod of Chalcis died, Berenice needed to frame her prospects in very different terms.

By the time of her second husband's death, after four years of marriage, Berenice had borne two sons, Berenicianus and Hyrcanus. The name of the first son, a masculinized form of Berenice, is unusual and conveys a sense of Queen Berenice's importance within her second marriage. The younger son's name came from the Maccabean side of the family. In naming their sons, Herod of Chalcis and Berenice unmistakably announced their success in the Herodian project of combining the Idumean and Maccabean lineages, indeed from both sides of the partnership; the names of the children were a declaration of both achievement and continuing ambition.

Herod of Chalcis had a son from a previous marriage, named Aristobulus, who could realistically contend for the inheritance of Chalcis, since he was also the product of an intra-Herodian marriage.[20] From the point of view of Berenice, however, her claim to the combined lineage was stronger, since Herod of Chalcis's first wife descended from Herod the Great's Samaritan wife, not from the Maccabean Mariamme. In any case Berenice was already resident in Chalcis as queen. Her decision to remain there with her sons, just as she reached her twentieth birthday, marked a transition in her influence.

With both Agrippa II and Aristobulus in Rome, and Tiberius Julius Alexander cycling out of the role of procurator, Claudius decided to opt for continuity by appointing Agrippa II in Chalcis, and at the same time to exert greater control in the region by appointing a more aggressive military commander in Judea, Ventidius Cumanus.[21] Crucially, Agrippa II also inherited authority over the Temple from Herod of Chalcis, who had recently appointed Ananias as high priest.

From the outset, Cumanus courted trouble in Jerusalem by bringing troops to the parapets around the Temple, some of whom engaged in taunting, obscene gestures. Rioting and confrontation were the predictable outcome, but bad turned to worse when soldiers felt licensed to plunder even outside Jerusalem.[22] Cumanus also accepted bribes from some Samaritans, to overlook their attack on some Galilean pilgrims making their way to the Temple, and the resultant communal violence made Tacitus portray the situation as bringing the province as a whole to the brink of war.[23] An appeal to Rome was authorized by the Syrian legate of the time, Ummidius

Quadratus, who had also decided to intervene militarily in an attempt to restore order. In Rome, Agrippa II interceded on behalf of the Temple, in which he had a key role, with both Claudius and Claudius's wife, Agrippina. Cumanus was removed and exiled. The new procurator, Felix, who was the brother of Claudius's trusted adviser Pallas, would attempt a new attitude in governance, although in the end his undoubted capacity for finesse proved unequal to the growing challenges of the period.[24]

Decisions in Rome were so vital to Agrippa II's fortunes that it is not surprising to find him mentioned more for what he did there than for what he did in Chalcis. It has been suggested that Agrippa II may never have actually taken up residence in the city of which he was titular king, but instead continued to lobby for what he in fact shortly received: a larger and more auspicious realm.[25] Two qualifications are in order, however. First, attempts to calculate durations of travel during the period, which are necessary to determine Agrippa II's whereabouts, cannot rise above notional estimates. Careful preparations were required for voyages; journey times varied with season, weather, and vagaries of the infrastructure of the time; and literary references to travel are notoriously romanticized. Second, Agrippa II has been depicted as a passive character, and in comparison to his sister that is understandable. But there is a tendency in the modern literature to exaggerate his passivity, and to draw conclusions from that biased assessment. During this period, whether present or absent, he could rely on the experience of his sister, only a year younger than he was, to see to Chalcis. The smooth functioning of governance there, always influenced and at least sometimes directed by Berenice, evidently impressed Claudius. Although he had declined to appoint Agrippa II immediately to take the place of his father in 44 CE, after his appointment to Chalcis, Agrippa II was appointed in 53 to be king in

Caesarea Philippi, exactly the position from which Agrippa I had made his remarkable ascent.[26] During the course of his shuffling of assignments, Claudius also conferred Chalcis on Aristobulus, thereby remaining loyal to the memories of both Agrippa I and Herod of Chalcis. Once again, the Herodians had demonstrated that imperial affection was one of their vital assets.

Agrippa II and Berenice both took up residence in Caesarea Philippi, which became for them a reliable fulcrum of power, especially because authority over the Temple in Jerusalem remained in Agrippa II's hands. Caesarea Philippi was the crowning achievement of Herod the Great's son Philip. The city had been known as Panias, after the god Pan. Philip, operating far from Jerusalem, leaned into the rich artistic diversity that his realm offered. Naming his capital after the emperor, Philip saw to it that the city, which functioned as a center for many differing cults and other devotions, offered a magnificent architectural setting for these diverse practices in proximity to his own royal palace.[27] Judaism, of course, was practiced by some subjects, but as one among many religions and practices. The fishing town of Bethsaida, far to the south, was a more typical setting for Judaic practice; from there, John 1:44 relates that two brothers named Andrew and Simon (later called Peter) came into contact with Jesus and were recruited to his movement.

Among the sons of Herod the Great who benefited from his last will and the favor of Augustus – Archelaus, Antipas, and Philip – perhaps the most successful was Philip, even if he was not the most ambitious. His building projects drew admiration and proved economically profitable; his propaganda for himself and the Romans, in architecture and in coins, was effective; his habit of touring his realm and dispensing justice gave him a reputation for even-handed adjudication; and his maintenance of security promoted trade.[28] Philip's Judaism was incidental to his rule, and unlike his brothers he even dropped the name "Herod" from his coins. A competent, diligent ruler, willing to compromise as well as to please, he was the rare example of a bland Herodian.

Philip left behind a well-regulated tetrarchy when he died in 34 CE, leading Gaius to place his realm under administrative jurisdiction as a holding measure until a plausible successor emerged. That successor would never be Antipas, despite his attempts to curry imperial favor; rather, Agrippa I began his meteoric trajectory with Caesarea Philippi as a result of his appointment there as king by Gaius. Berenice had become familiar with the city as a betrothed girl prior to taking up residence in Alexandria with Marcus Julius Alexander. As a young child she had already come to know Tiberias, but Caesarea Philippi was where she first became aware of herself as belonging to the most important family in the region. Agrippa II might also have become familiar with the place at that time, although he was based more in Rome than anywhere else during the bulk of his father's rule. In any case, compared to Rome itself or Alexandria (another preeminent city of the empire), Philip's capital, however ornate and multicultural, did not rank as a cosmopolitan center.

Within the sacred geography of the former realm of Herod the Great, which was centered on Jerusalem, Caesarea Philippi, far north of the Sea of Galilee and to its east, also appears peripheral. But during a period in which Claudius felt secure only with a procurator in charge of Judea, Samaria, Galilee, and Perea, the fact that he assigned Gaulanitis and its associated lands to Agrippa II was a notable indication of confidence. To extend beyond that territory and fully take over the inheritance of their father, Agrippa II and Berenice would need not only to execute policies that assured good governance, but also to leverage the cycle of wealth that Philip had put in place and to intervene cleverly within the imperial court.

Berenice had already proven adept at governance in Chalcis after the death of her husband Herod of Chalcis; Agrippa II was well established in Rome as an accomplished courtier; and they both would deftly exploit the wealth of Caesarea Philippi to make patronage a cornerstone of their advancement.

Although Aristobulus had been considerately handled, and would go on to a successful career within the Roman Empire, Claudius's treatment showed that even after his death, Agrippa I – and therefore his surviving family – remained an imperial favorite. Berenice and her sons naturally followed Agrippa II to Caesarea Philippi, departing from Chalcis and leaving the way clear for Aristobulus to take up his responsibilities. As long as her brother Agrippa II remained unmarried and childless, and continued to be the most prominent and the most favored Herodian heir, she could reasonably hope that her young sons, Berenicianus and Hyrcanus, might be considered natural inheritors of the dynastic project. Once, Agrippa I had parlayed his appointment in Caesarea Philippi to acquire the entire realm of Herod the Great. His untimely death had put the inheritance of that achievement in doubt. But now, with Agrippa I's son in Caesarea Philippi and his nephew in Chalcis, the possibility of recovery was reawakened. For Berenice, her brother offered the immediate prospect of security and influence, while her sons represented the potential of power on a scale that few Herodian women had exerted.

For ambition on that scale to succeed, however, the violence in Judea and Samaria that Cumanus had exacerbated would need to be addressed. Cumanus had been venal and brutal, while Felix brought competence, connections at court, and a taste for intrigue to this new office. But any procurator faced increasing levels of apparently spontaneous rioting, physical aggression, and planned attacks between factions and on Roman soldiers. Once the pattern showed itself in the heartland of Herod the Great's former territory, its extension into neighboring territories, especially Galilee and Perea but also Gaulanitis, was all too predictable. If Agrippa II and Berenice wished to hold on to what they had managed to secure – with a remarkably efficient combination of competence on her part and lobbying on his part – they would need to establish an efficient relationship with the procurator. Their authority and influence over the Temple provided a plausible foundation for such a relationship, but the relationship itself remained to be established. If that could be put in place, and Judea and Samaria came at last to be pacified, then perhaps Berenice's brother, and after him even one of her sons, would one day sit on the throne of Herod the Great.

CHAPTER FOUR

Wife of King Polemon

Shortly after Berenice and Agrippa II took up residence in Caesarea Philippi, Claudius died. A convoluted plot, attested to among later historians, intimates that his wife, Agrippina, hastened his death by poison in order to see to the accession of her son Nero, although Josephus and Suetonius are less sure of that scenario.[1] Whatever the merits of the claim, Agrippina was a granddaughter of Antonia, whose support had been important to Agrippa I. To keep a degree of maneuverability within the court, then, and ideally enhance his position, Agrippa II began to invest a precious share of his family's personal capital: his sisters.

Marriages among client kings had long been encouraged by the imperial court. Herod the Great's son Archelaus had married the Cappadocian princess Glaphyra, although this did not enable him to survive the consequences of violence in Judea and his own incompetence. Indeed, that marriage exacerbated Archelaus's difficulties, because Glaphyra was the widow of his half-brother Alexander.[2] That put him at odds with pious opinion, as was later the case in John the Baptist's criticism of Antipas's marriage to Herodias. Agrippa II, however, put marital arrangements to more adept use as an instrument of policy, by means of his sisters. Berenice, the eldest sister, was both part of the execution of the policy and one of its authors.

Of all the marriages concerned, Drusilla offered the dynasty the most immediate advantage, albeit by a convoluted path. In 53 CE she married Azizus, the king of Emesa (a principality north of Chalcis), another of Rome's client-rulers. Neither Azizus nor most people in his kingdom were practitioners of Judaism, yet he accepted circumcision prior to the marriage. This was a requirement that Herodian women before and after Drusilla insisted on, and constitutes a striking feature of their marital policy. Earlier, Drusilla had been promised to Epiphanes, son of King Antiochus of Commagene (a region even farther north than Emesa), but he did not adhere to his agreement to accept circumcision, so the promise of marriage became moot. Despite Azizus's willingness to accept circumcision, his marriage with Drusilla did not last, and it was Drusilla, Josephus reports, who ended the relationship.[3] So in addition to demanding circumcision of their would-be husbands, Herodian women – Berenice included, as will emerge – arrogated to themselves the right to divorce. That pattern is persistent enough to require discussion, but Drusilla's trajectory at this time demands more immediate attention.

In a strange story, told as an aside, Josephus describes a meeting between Drusilla and Felix, the newly appointed procurator. After the meeting, Felix was smitten to the point that he had one of his friends, a Cypriote Jew, impersonate a magician to try to persuade Drusilla to abandon Azizus and become Felix's wife. The story accords with Felix's reputation for duplicity and self-indulgence in the presentation of Tacitus.[4] Drusilla agreed to marry Felix, and they eventually had a son, named Agrippa. The intervention of the pseudo-magician is a bizarre feature of Josephus's tale, yet it fits his negative attitude toward Herodian women as liable to fall prey to all manner of charms. By any political reckoning, however, the marriage represented a coup for the Herodian dynasty, aligning its interests with those of the procurator in a way that went beyond even its influence on Tiberius Julius Alexander. Drusilla had redirected her marital capital, exchanging an alliance north with Syrian royalty for the ability to exert direct influence on the procurator in Judea, and the result was a considerable advance for her and her family.

Felix offered Judea a degree of stability, serving nearly to the end of the decade, and he flaunted his Herodian connection by incorporating on his coinage a symbol of Herod the Great: crossed palm branches.[5] The book of Acts 24:24 also mentions Drusilla as Felix's wife at the time he investigated the apostle Paul and the case against him, identifying her as a Judean but failing to mention her Herodian connection or even that Berenice, who appears in the next sequence in Acts 25:13–27, was her sister. Although Acts does not accord Drusilla her due, the marriage was more durable than her first, the Herodian dynasty was strengthened, Roman rule in Judea showed signs of benefiting from its alliance with the family, and Felix profited from his association with the Herodians – though Felix's taste for profit, unfortunately, would undo much of what he was able to accomplish.

Herodian women's demand for circumcision as a requirement for marriage and their initiation of divorces, however, drew attention even in the ancient period. Josephus mentions divorce in connection with the sister of Herod the Great, Salome, whom he characterizes as an intriguer of the first order. He reports that she sent her husband, Costabarus, a writ of divorce, "which was not in accordance with Jewish law."[6] In making that claim, Josephus agrees with later Rabbinic practice, but in fact, while the Second Temple stood, the ethos surrounding divorce in Judaism was more diverse. Discussion of whether women could divorce their husbands in recent literature has been vigorous, but whatever one thinks of the practice, it was a fact on the ground, represented in texts going back to the fifth century BCE and reflected in the marital histories of Salome and her great-grandnieces Drusilla and, as will emerge, Berenice. Their practice was far from universal, but it was current.[7]

After Salome's divorce, she denounced Costabarus to her brother for plotting against him, and Herod the Great had him executed. (A similar fate had also befallen Salome's first husband.) When she then expressed the desire to marry a third time, her brother proceeded cautiously. Syllaeus, the would-be groom and minister of the neighboring Nabatean kingdom, approached Herod himself with a proposal of marriage, but was disappointed to learn that he would first need to accept circumcision.[8] Syllaeus complained with regret that he feared he would be stoned to death if he converted to Judaism, and despite his passion and Salome's, there was no marriage. Salome would move on, and later marry someone else. The pattern in regard to Herodian women insisting on circumcision for marriage with a gentile is plain.

The thinking behind the insistence is not conveyed in Josephus's report, although it may relate to the conflicted story of Dinah and Shechem in the book of Genesis 34:1–31. In that narrative, Shechem rapes Dinah, then approaches her family to marry her. When all the males of Shechem's city agree to circumcision as a condition of the marriage, two of Jacob's sons take advantage of the opportunity to attack them as they are recuperating, and put them to the sword. The precedent may seem strained as a justification for the behavior of several Herodian women, but the narrative deals with the issue of circumcision in relation to outsiders, and the Herodian family did engage in religious argument.[9] Herod the Great himself was known to defend his conduct from religious objections, on one occasion insisting in an elaborate public demonstration that, because trophies he had set up in connection with athletic events in Jerusalem were obviously nothing more than bits of wood with coverings of cloth, they were not idols.[10] The king's argument, more rhetorical than cogent, carried the day in Josephus's telling, but since it was followed by attempts to assassinate him, the king's performance art had obviously not triumphed. His and the Herodians' arguments in regard to women divorcing their husbands and the deployment of circumcision to facilitate intermarriage may or may not have convinced many other practitioners of Judaism, whatever precisely those arguments were, but those practices are persistent features of the Herodian's own Judaic ethos.

The pattern set by Salome was also partially represented by the middle daughter of Agrippa I, Mariamme. Her father had promised her to the son of a family with a long-standing association with the Herodians when she was only ten years old, the same age at which Berenice had been betrothed to Marcus Julius Alexander. Agrippa II stood by the betrothal, and Mariamme duly married Archelaus, the son of Helcias, bearing a daughter whom she touchingly named Berenice.[11] But that marriage did not last. Mariamme divorced Archelaus, marrying instead Demetrius, who had been appointed the alabarch in Alexandria, and bearing a son named Agrippinus. In this way, Mariamme enhanced a long-standing relationship with the alabarchate and reinforced financial ties with Alexandria, a connection that would become increasingly important to Agrippa II and Berenice over time, as their grip over their own lands was weakened from the growing violence of insurrection. In Mariamme's case, Demetrius was Jewish by birth and practiced as a Jew, so the issue of circumcision did not arise, although divorce had been necessary to contract the marriage.

Josephus appears bemused by Herodian women's propensity to divorce and by their strictness in regard to circumcision. But his own horizon for the practice of Judaism was more limited than he wanted his audience to think. His often repeated description of the four schools of Judaism – priestly, Pharisaic, Essene, and revolutionary – refers to practices and concepts in Judea, and especially the vicinity of Jerusalem. He even claims to have mastered the major teachings involved in all of the schools by way of passing himself off as an expert in Judaism as a whole.[12] In the world of the diaspora, however, Judaism adapted to the particular environments involved, evolving forms of religion that are not fully documented. An example already mentioned is that Philo of Alexandria had portrayed the practice of circumcising male children as not merely a literal practice, but also an enactment of cutting away passions from intellectual discernment, which Philo saw as the goal of both Moses and his philosophical hero Plato. That opened the prospect that circumcision might be seen as symbolic, so that the physical act should not be required. Because circumcision was commonly ridiculed within the Roman Empire, Philo felt the need to resist that claim.[13]

The possibility of symbolic circumcision was especially attractive to a particular group of people, referred to in literary sources as well as inscriptions, who admired the monotheism of Judaism and its portrayal of God as an ethical force; attended and supported synagogues; and kept other practices of the religion – short of circumcision. One member of this group, a Roman soldier named Cornelius in the book of Acts, is characterized in these terms. He is portrayed as an early and pivotal contact for the apostle Peter in Acts, chapter 10, and serves to emphasize the importance of the entire group of "God-fearers," as these gentiles were called, among the surprising new constituencies that Jesus's movement developed after his resurrection. Philo probably died during the 40s CE, before Christianity became a force to be reckoned with in the diaspora, yet he did have to contend with the thought that circumcision should be considered superfluous as a literal practice. That became an issue all the more with the rise of Christianity, even as a movement with limited impact.

By the 50s, the letters of the apostle Paul had begun to circulate in Greek; his position relativized the importance of some ritual practices. Especially in his Letter to the Galatians, Paul specifically opposed requiring circumcision for gentiles who had come to believe in Christ and wished to accept baptism. The earlier contact of the Herodian dynasty with Jesus, during the time of Antipas in Galilee and Pontius Pilate in Judea, had not been in the least friendly, but the issues then did not include the integration of non-Jews by means of baptism, a shift of practice among Jesus's followers after his death that the narrative in regard to Cornelius is intended to mark. Both Drusilla and, as will emerge in this chapter, Berenice had contact with Paul. But whether or not they became specifically aware of Paul's activity and thought, Agrippa I's daughters, in their insistence on circumcision, moved in a diametrically opposite direction to a robust strand in earliest Christianity.

Indeed, Drusilla, although she eventually married Felix – who naturally, as a Roman official, did not submit to the requirement of circumcision – was involved from an early age in insisting on the practice. She was just six years old when Agrippa I died and she was promised in marriage to Epiphanes, son of the king of Commagene. Clearly, parents were the moving forces in such agreements, and circumcision was a matter of Herodian marital policy, such that each of the daughters involved acted more as an agent of the dynasty than as an individual with preferences. Nonetheless, each of them was involved in executing the insistence on circumcision, which as a whole is reminiscent of the ancient Maccabean program of requiring the practice within lands that they had conquered. Just as the precise thinking behind the insistence on circumcision by the Herodians is not detailed, so the glaring exception to this rule in the case of Drusilla's marriage to Felix remains unexplained. As a practical matter, attempting to require a Roman procurator to circumcise prior to marriage would have been a vain effort, but the relaxation of the requirement might also reflect an understanding of the Romans as representing a different kind of gentile. The comparison of Rome with Esau, the brother of Jacob, which was emerging during this period, opens this possibility to consideration.[14] Whatever argument may or may not have been involved, Drusilla set a precedent that would prove crucial to the last and most famous liaison of Berenice's life.

Berenice herself, the eldest sister involved in the policy of the family, contracted a marriage that also required the circumcision of the husband-to-be. The groom was Polemon, king of Pontus, Colchis, and Cilicia in Asia Minor. The peculiar fashion in which Josephus chooses to relate the events concerning the marriage have exerted a formative influence on the way Berenice has been remembered as a person, but the incidents involved seem clear, and well within Herodian marital policy as a whole.[15] She entered the marriage after having been twice widowed. In her twenties and in the process of raising two sons, she continued to embrace the practice of contracting useful marriages for the dynasty, while insisting on the emblematic ritual of Judaism that her sister Drusilla had upheld in her first marriage.

Because Polemon is referred to by Josephus as the king of Cilicia, it has been argued that the marriage must have occurred sometime after 63 CE.[16] By that time, Nero had reduced Polemon's realm, depriving him of Pontus and Colchis, which were attached to a province directly under Roman rule, and leaving him with Cilicia alone. There are a couple of problems with that chronology. On Polemon's side, by the 60s he was using his coinage to celebrate his marriage to a different wife altogether, Julia Mamaea, so his marriage to Berenice must have been over and done with by that time. On Berenice's side, her presence not in Polemon's realms but in Jerusalem was especially intense during the early 60s. When Josephus refers to Polemon as king of Cilicia, he is indeed writing from the perspective of after Polemon's demotion, because he published his *Antiquities* during the winter of 93–94. His perspective, however, is evidently not the same as the timeframe of the marriage. It would have been strange if Berenice, by this time acting on her own behalf and no longer under the tutelage of her father, undertook a marriage at the exact moment that her groom was being deprived of lands. Such a course would not be in character for her, for Agrippa I during his lifetime, or for Agrippa II. She, after all, had previously, with Marcus Julius Alexander, married into one of the wealthiest families in Egypt, and then with Herod of Chalcis married within Herodian royalty. She was and remained a queen, and needed a good reason to depart from Caesarea Philippi.

The fullest extent of the lands ruled by Polemon – Pontus and Colchis as well as Cilicia – amounted to such a reason. In addition, Polemon was descended from Mark Antony, who had deep associations with the region. When Cleopatra sailed up the Cydnus River to greet Antony, the events as described took place in Cilician Tarsus, which was also the natal city of the apostle Paul. The location of Polemon's realm made it wealthy: it was close to trading routes, the Mediterranean as well as the Black Sea, and included mining resources as well as agriculture. Adding its wealth to Herodian collaterals was an excellent move, and a characteristic one for Berenice and Agrippa II. She planned the marriage after having successfully helped to place both Mariamme and Drusilla. When precisely she married Polemon cannot be determined. Josephus writes only that she remarried after being a widow for "much time" after Herod of Chalcis's death in 48 CE. Taking that vague statement into account with the other chronological considerations would suggest that she was married again prior to her thirtieth birthday, perhaps in 56. With that arrangement in place, the daughters of Agrippa I would have done as much for the dynasty as Agrippa II had. Drusilla provided access to the procurator of Judea, Mariamme to the financing of Egypt, and Berenice to the wealth and power of Pontus, Colchis, and Cilicia. Berenice, too, supplied the essential male heirs from Herod of Chalcis, her sons Berenicianus and Hyrcanus.

However profitable the marriage may have seemed to the family in prospect, Berenice still insisted on Polemon's circumcision, and he complied. Of the duration of the marriage, Josephus says only that it did not last long. That seems correct, in that Berenice was active on her own again back in Caesarea Philippi and Jerusalem within the decade. At the end of a comparatively brief interval, she left Polemon and returned to her brother. She was leaving a great deal behind. By way of explanation, Josephus remarks that she left "on account of dissoluteness."[17] He does not indicate whose dissipation he has in mind, although contextually he goes out of his way to portray Berenice as undisciplined and profligate in the extreme. Josephus's narrative concerning Berenice's character and behavior needs to be taken into account before his mention of "dissoluteness" being the cause of the breakup of the marriage with Polemon can be assessed.

By the time he came to write his *Antiquities*, Josephus was actively promulgating the gossip, likely the inspiration behind Juvenal's satire, that Berenice and Agrippa II were involved in an incestuous relationship.[18] In the case of her agreement to marry Polemon, Josephus even asserts that Berenice pursued the marriage because she wanted to give the lie to the rumor about Agrippa II and herself by marrying someone else. This portrait of cynicism is further elaborated by the claim that Polemon agreed to the union in view of her wealth. No doubt Berenice by this stage was independently wealthy, but the basis of that wealth – inherited lands, plantations, and buildings of her family – could not travel with her from Caesarea Philippi to Asia Minor. Polemon's resources were in any case greater than hers, or Agrippa II's, at the time of the marriage. Josephus's remark about Polemon's motivation is malicious to the point of being implausible.

Animosity toward Berenice is not limited in Josephus's description to references to incest and to marrying for money. Just before writing of this marriage, while describing Drusilla's marital adventures, Josephus notes that Drusilla agreed "to transgress the ancestral laws" and marry Felix because Berenice had been mistreating Drusilla, jealous of Drusilla's beauty.[19] Here again, the only thing more glaring than Josephus's malicious intent is his lack of plausibility. By this stage in his own narrative, Drusilla has been subjected to quasi-magical intervention as well as ordinary seduction by Felix. On top of that, she has been married to Azizus, whom she divorced to accept Felix's offer – that is, she was hardly sequestered with her sister in Caesarea Philippi. Trying to portray Drusilla as an innocent held hostage by her older sister's jealousy and, in effect, compelled to break with the policy of requiring the circumcision of a future husband makes no more sense in terms of Drusilla's behavior than it does for Berenice's. They both made advantageous marriages for the benefit of their dynastic family and for themselves – Drusilla by breaking with their usual pattern in regard to circumcision, and Berenice by upholding it.

The reasons that Josephus depicted Berenice and Drusilla in this way, and at this point (by the time Josephus wrote his *Antiq-*

uities), become clear only in the light of later events. His motivations come into focus within the context of the radically changed situation after the destruction of the Second Temple in 70, and his particular intentions will need to be taken up at a later stage, when Berenice in Rome pursued an agenda that was, ironically, similar to his in some ways, and yet at odds with the strategy he preferred. For the moment, the concern is only to identify how tendentious his presentation is. Indeed, it has been suggested that he here incorporates a separate, anti-Herodian or anti-Berenicean, source, one intent on vilifying Herodian women as profligate, cruel to future husbands, and arrogant in acting against Jewish law.[20] The pattern already identified, centered on practices of women compelling circumcision and divorcing their husbands, is cited as evidence for this hypothesis. But because the presentations are formulaic and deliberately scandalizing, they may also be seen as tropes rather than sources, literary reflexes triggered in Josephus's writing by the process of characterizing Herodian women in negative terms.

When Josephus writes about "dissoluteness" breaking up the marriage between Polemon and Berenice, therefore, and does not actually specify that it was on her part, that opens the possibility that Polemon's behavior, not hers, was licentious and that as a result Berenice divorced him. Only Josephus's pattern of presenting Herodian women supports the idea that Berenice was acting on some supposedly uncontrollable incestuous desire, and he no doubt would have been happy for his audience to draw that inference. But bad conduct by Polemon would better account for her behavior than the supposition that Berenice, having decided to leave an incestuous relationship behind her, belatedly came to the conclusion that she could not do without sexual intercourse with her brother. She was after all nearly thirty years old, well experienced sexually, and in the midst of her third marriage. More likely, something untoward and unanticipated motivated her departure.

Of Polemon himself, Josephus observes that Berenice's departure released him both from the marriage and from abiding by the customs of Judaism, as if the two were equally burdensome to him.[21] The remark suggests that Josephus realized that Polemon's accommodation to Judaism, despite his personal sacrifice, had been far from comprehensive, and that marriage – or, at least, faithfulness to Berenice within marriage – did not suit him. In any case, by the 60s, a few short years after Berenice's departure, Polemon was striking coins to acclaim his new wife, Julia Mamaea from Emesa, as queen of the realm of which he was the "great king."[22] However disagreeable his behavior with Berenice had been, by departing that marriage she avoided his demotion under Nero, just when her presence in Jerusalem became critical. Still, the failure of the marriage represented a failure on her part within the Herodian stratagem. A fresh initiative was called for, and she did not delay in positioning herself within a new pattern of activity altogether.

Berenice's return to Caesarea Philippi corresponded to a period of mounting tension in the region, emanating from Jerusalem. To some extent, the growth of conflict had inadvertently been exacerbated by the policies of Felix. He resorted to violence as a matter of policy, as Tacitus remarks.[23] He entered into an extensive dispute with the high priest Jonathan, which he decided to resolve by having Jonathan murdered. Felix executed his plan by hiring a group of *sicarii,* "dagger-men," assassins who concealed their weapons within their clothing and operated in broad daylight anywhere they liked in Jerusalem, according to Josephus, including in the Temple.[24] Recourse to these killers, whether by the procurator or priestly factions, would gradually render Jerusalem ungovernable; Josephus even writes that from that point God no longer regarded the Temple as a sufficiently pure place for his presence, desecrated as it was by human bloodshed.

Agrippa II did what he could by appointing a new high priest. By this point, however, a factional ethos had become established in Jerusalem that proved disastrous within the history of the Second Temple. The agreement among diverse interests that had enabled Jerusalem to thrive gave way to strife among procurators, high priests, priests, anti-Roman agitators, partisans of exclusive views of Judaism (such as Pharisees and Essenes), and the populace at large.[25] Wealthy groups were capable of contracting their own sicarii and pillaging one another, and some did so as a matter of course. Felix was called back to Rome at the end of the decade; violence had become the undeniable order of the day, and only the fact that he was the brother of Pallas saved him from difficulty in the imperial court.[26] Yet at the same time, the Temple functioned in the eyes of most practitioners of Judaism in the known world as the single place on earth where God was pleased to accept sacrifice and confirm his covenant with his people. In the face of mounting violence, a more peaceful alternative emerged out of that conviction, and Berenice became one of its principal champions.

The example of Agrippa I in supporting those who wished to offer Nazirite vows was not isolated.[27] Queen Helena of Adiabene is said by Josephus to have engaged in lavish generosity at the time of the famine in 46 CE, and the Mishnah recounts her personally fulfilling the vow when her son returned safely from war.[28] A burial cave discovered in 1967 attests to the pride of a family in its Nazirite practice during the same period.[29] Because the vow was not a requirement, but a self-offering that a man or woman took on as a matter of personal volition, it distinguished itself from other practices in the Temple. A person who engaged in the practice deliberately abstained from impurity during a period set at the beginning of the vow, and appeared with sacrifices for the Temple as a personal specimen of purity, whose very hair was consecrated and presented to God as an offering at the altar. The stipulated sacrifices themselves were both favored by God and expensive, so donors who sponsored Nazirite vows, such as Agrippa I had done, were also singled out for praise. Particularly at a time when those charged with keeping the good order of sacrifice were engaging in violence, the example of the Nazirites and their sponsors was a solace, as well as a wordless appeal to God and adherents of Judaism for good order and harmony.

Agrippa II and Berenice were directly involved in helping to resolve a dispute in the Temple in regard to Nazirite practice. After they had done so, Berenice herself took on a Nazirite vow at a moment of critical conflict concerning the Temple, a period discussed in Chapter 5. It is commonly agreed that her intervention in Jerusalem at that moment represents the most dramatic act of her life. Understanding what she did involves appreciating why such vows were valued, and analyzing how Berenice adjudicated the value of Nazirite vows offers insight into her own actions. In the process of tracing her development in this regard, a revision in Herodian policy toward Christianity also becomes apparent.

Given the apostle Paul's reputation as an opponent of Jewish law, it will come as a surprise to some readers that he became involved in Nazirite practice in Jerusalem. He did precisely that, however, and the result of his actions brought him into contact with Agrippa II and Berenice. What led him to that point was in fact a persistent outworking of his own position, developed since the time of his conversion in 32. From the moment that he declared God's risen Son had been revealed within him, his stated apostolic purpose was to announce Christ among non-Jews, or gentiles, as he writes in his Letter to the Galatians 1:13–17. In his programmatic practice, the gentiles who received that announcement with faith were to be baptized in Jesus's name, but keeping the whole of the Torah of Moses was not to be imposed as an additional requirement on them. Like God-fearers, they remained gentiles in regard to circumcision, even as baptism made them part of God's chosen people. Paul also insisted, however, that Jews who believed in Jesus were included in the full community he describes in his Letter to the Romans 11:26, where he writes that "all Israel will be saved." That is, both practicing Jews for whom the Torah pointed the way to faith and gentiles who shared that faith were part of an enhanced version of the chosen people: "all Israel." Those words were a part of his letter to communities of those who believed in Jesus in Rome, which he wrote in 57, setting out the itinerary that would bring about his meeting with Agrippa II and Berenice.

Paul declares in his Letter to the Romans 15:23–33 his plans to come to Rome, which he had not yet visited, after completing a sacrifice in Jerusalem on behalf of the predominantly gentile communities he had founded in the northern arc of the Roman Empire. They had been generous in providing him with funds, so that he could use those resources to secure offerings that he could present within the Temple as a practicing Jew. Indeed, Paul's letters include references to his deliberate program of collecting funds for this purpose.[30] His plan was to bring into the Temple a tangible example of his vision of "all Israel," a united sacrifice of Jews and gentiles who believed in Jesus as the Son of God.

Paul made two assumptions in conceiving his plan, which effected a strategy many years in the making. First, he assumed that, as in the case of the daily sacrifices offered in the name of the emperor, it was perfectly acceptable for gentiles to donate offerings, provided they did not personally enter into the Sanctuary, which was restricted to Israelites. Second, the continuing accessibility of the Temple for those engaged in Nazirite practice was taken for granted. This is reflected in Paul having his head shaved on the way to Jerusalem, so that he could keep his own vow in the interim until he could be shaved again, and present his hair in Jerusalem as a Nazirite.[31]

In Jerusalem, Paul in fact found, and no doubt knew that he would find, a small but robust community of Nazirites who were also dedicated to a belief in Jesus. Their leader was James, the brother of Jesus, who as described in the book of Acts 21:17–26 had emerged as the most prestigious figure of the movement in Jerusalem. Four members of this community were already fully prepared to be presented as Nazirites in the Temple at the completion of the period of their vow.[32] Paul could easily associate with them, pay for their sacrifices, and so smoothly integrate his own "offering of the gentiles," as he called it in Romans 15:16, within the regular conduct of worship in the Temple.

The plan was upset by the rise of factionalism in Jerusalem as well as by Paul's reputation. As priestly factions gained power, some of them resisted accepting gifts from gentiles in the Temple, including offerings such as Paul's. Resistance to such gifts was not yet to the point where offerings in the name of the emperor were being refused, but it would be one day – and explosively so. Even at this stage, however, it is likely that knowledge of where Paul's funding derived from disturbed his reception in Jerusalem. Worse, just as today many people think that Paul adhered to a denial of the validity of the Law of Moses for all practitioners, including Jews, in his own time this misunderstanding was prevalent as well. As a result, when he and his group of Nazirites entered the Temple ready to complete their act of sanctification, the rumor spread among other worshippers there that Paul was in fact introducing gentiles into the most sacred precincts of the complex, which were prohibited to gentiles. Had this been true, it would have been a deliberate act of pollution; even the Roman authorities agreed that death was a suitable punishment for a gentile who infringed the area of the Sanctuary.[33]

Predictably, given the febrile religio-political atmosphere in Jerusalem at that time, and particularly in the Temple, a riot broke out in the area near the Sanctuary. A small force of Romans was garrisoned adjacent to the Temple in the fortress called the Antonia, which Herod the Great had dedicated in honor of Mark Antony. They intervened in the melee, and the book of Acts gives an account of a lengthy, well-composed speech that Paul gave in his own defense, which is no doubt an idealized version of events. Acts 21:33–23:35 goes on to detail an assassination attempt against Paul's life, after a fruitless attempt by the Roman officer Claudius Lysias to resolve the matter by means of the Jerusalem council, the Sanhedrin. Faced with the twin difficulties that Paul, as a citizen of Tarsus, had the benefits of Roman citizenship, including the right of a proper hearing, and that the level of violence directed against him did not appear controllable, Claudius Lysias dispatched Paul to Caesarea Maritima, so that the procurator Felix could deal with the matter directly.

Felix reacted by convening a session with Paul and the high priest Ananias, who came with an attorney named Tertullus. Tertullus shifted the ground of a charge against Paul by accusing all his ilk with insurrection. Felix prevaricated, eventually involving his wife Drusilla in his interrogation of the prisoner (according to Acts 24:1–26). House arrest in Caesarea Maritima was the immediate result of a combination of Felix's uncertainty and his hope for financial benefit from Paul's supporters.

Felix played interests against one another on several occasions in order to gain financially. When violence broke out in Caesarea Maritima between Jews and Syrians, the broad license he gave to troops he brought from Syria resulted in the looting, rape, destruction, and murder of some of the Jewish community. The outrage was reported in Rome, and Felix was recalled.[34] His successor, Porcius Festus, had little preparation to deal with the case of Paul, and he at first fell back on the methods of Claudius Lysias and Felix, by convening a meeting with Paul's priestly opponents. They appealed to Festus to have Paul sent back to Jerusalem, where their intent was to kill him. Understanding the danger, Paul invoked his rights as a citizen to appeal to Caesar (Acts 25:1–12).

That was the setting in which Agrippa II and Berenice made their way to Caesarea Maritima, in order to welcome Festus into his new appointment. As a courtesy to them, and no doubt out of genuine perplexity, the procurator had them meet and hear out Paul, as is recounted in Acts 25:13–26:32. The narrative of Acts attributes to Paul a fulsome account of his position, as is also afforded him earlier, but its conclusion laconically reveals a key change in the Herodian view of Jesus and his followers as a result of the involvement of Agrippa II and Berenice. A generation before, their relative Antipas had ordered the execution of John the Baptist, had sought to eliminate Jesus (Luke 13:31), and had consulted with Pontius Pilate in the Pilate's decision to crucify Jesus (23:1–12). Their own father had been present when Claudius made his decision against Jewish believers in Jesus in Rome, and he had ordered the beheading of James, the son of Zebedee. In the case of Paul, however, no Herodian intervention against Jesus's movement emerged. Acts even describes the Herodian attitude as turning into a degree of sympathy, by having Agrippa II quip to Paul in Acts 26:28 that he is so convincing as to be on the brink of turning him into a Christian. But in this same cycle of narrative, even Felix is credited in

Acts 24:22 with accurate knowledge of the new faith, which does not seem plausible in light of his actions.

Yet in the midst of the growing chaos and violence, centered in the Temple but now also swirling out to reach Caesarea Maritima, Agrippa II and Berenice made a balanced suggestion when confronted with the case of Paul. Whatever resentment had motivated Antipas in the cases of John the Baptist and Jesus, whatever advantage Claudius and Agrippa I had seen in exploiting the differences between Jewish believers in Jesus and other Jews, Agrippa II and Berenice realized that the direct devotion to the Temple represented by the Nazirite vow had long been a unifying element in the practice of Judaism. Their father had sponsored Nazirites, and Agrippa II and Berenice knew of prominent people and families who had made the vow into a means of expressing their dedication to the ancestral ways while at the same time enhancing their own status and prestige. At a time when factionalism and resort to sicarii gangs by procurators and priestly groups alike threatened to make Jerusalem and Judea as a whole ungovernable, pious acts that could be commended, no matter who performed them, increased in value for anyone concerned with the stability and peace of Jerusalem. Agrippa II and Berenice both shared that concern, and Berenice especially would later see the peaceful power that the Nazirite vow could exert in a violent world, and make it her own. As they consulted with Porcius Festus (Acts 26:30–32), they shared the conclusion that Paul might have been released, but his appeal to be tried in Rome, as a citizen, made that city his ineluctable destination.

Although Berenice is clearly identified in Acts in this crucial shift of the Herodian position (with Drusilla also in the background), she is not given a voice in the narrative any way like Agrippa II, Felix, Festus, and especially Paul are. Even Paul's male opponents have much to say, but not Berenice. She is mute in this book of the New

Testament, and no more loquacious in Josephus's works, where she negotiates the hectic events of the period that made her a widow, a queen, a mother, a widow again, a wife who divorced her husband, and a counselor to her brother the king as he attempted to recover from the premature death of their father – all without saying anything. That imposed silence is a reminder that the sources at our disposal do us no favors as we try to understand Berenice's motivations. Fortunately, her actions, when placed in their immediate contexts, speak eloquently of her intents.

PART III

Imperial Consort

CHAPTER FIVE

Penitent in Jerusalem

After they made themselves useful to the new procurator by advising what to do about the apostle Paul, Agrippa II and Berenice strategically cultivated a relationship with Porcius Festus. They had fewer inroads than with previous procurators – they did not have the family connection that Drusilla had forged with Felix, or that Berenice had had with Tiberius Julius Alexander at an earlier stage – but they did share with the new procurator a concern to address the violence that was gripping Jerusalem. Sicarii were routinely active, to the extent that high priestly and priestly factions were engaged in mutual campaigns of assassination. Festus responded by sending out security forces, rather than by enlisting sicarii of his own, and the change of policy was wise, complementing a move by Agrippa II and Berenice to exert greater control over the conduct of the Temple.[1]

Agrippa II used the authority he had inherited from Herod of Chalcis to appoint a new high priest, Ishmael ben Phabi, a move that diminished the influence of Ananias, the high priest who had opposed the apostle Paul's Nazirite claims.[2] In addition, as the extensive program of renovating and extending the Temple that Herod the Great had begun was coming to a close, Agrippa II made a fateful change to the surrounding architecture. Transparently, the intent was to assert Herodian influence over the Temple. To the west of the Temple, Herod the Great had characteristically extended and fortified a Maccabean palace to serve as his own. This was the home base for Agrippa II and Berenice when they were in Jerusalem. The height of the palace already offered it a magnificent view of the city as a whole; Agrippa improved on that by erecting a high platform, serving as a dining room, that let him observe activities within the Sanctuary of the Temple.

Josephus, always sympathetic to Agrippa II, describes the king's pleasure in taking his meals there, overlooking the sacrifices as he reclined in what was clearly constructed to be an observatory.[3] Authorities in the Temple took a much dimmer view of the new building project, and evidently of Agrippa II himself. They responded by answering construction with construction, building up a high wall on the Temple's west side in order to obstruct Agrippa II's view. This new project also obstructed ordinary Roman surveillance of the vast exterior court of the Temple, and so posed a risk to security in the view of Porcius Festus. Accordingly, Festus ordered the wall demolished, in what was not only a victory for Agrippa II and Berenice, but also a visible indication of their successful alliance with the procurator.

Had the matter ended there, it might have signaled a revival of the effectiveness of the Roman-Herodian collaboration. The priests, however, had other ideas. In an ominous portent of the rapid collapse to come, Ishmael ben Phabi, whom Agrippa II had appointed to be high priest, joined in the objection to Festus's order, petitioning for the procurator to let them send an embassy to Nero in Rome.[4] Their grounds were that they could not countenance the destruction of even a portion of the Temple – although the wall in question had been their own recent construction. Priestly defense of the Temple, then, was emerging as a principle that alleged a right of priestly autonomy in Jerusalem, carrying implications for governance throughout Judea. Because the Temple stood at the center of Rome's policy concerning Judea and its relationship to the large Jewish population throughout the empire, Festus had little choice but to authorize the embassy, so a delegation that included Ishmael and ten other dignitaries made its way to Rome.

Nero could easily have endorsed the command of his procurator, on the grounds that it was a matter of security not to interfere with Roman surveillance of the Temple. Alternatively, he might have agreed to sponsor a negotiation over the legitimacy of the Herodian observatory in comparison with the priestly obstruction. But the emperor did neither of those things. Instead, he reversed Festus's decision, and ruled that the new Temple wall erected by the priests should stand. Josephus attributes Nero's decision to the influence of Poppaea, at the time Nero's mistress and soon to be his wife, whom Josephus also describes as a worshipper of God, another term for a God-fearer.[5] Given Poppaea's long and intimate involvement with Roman imperial politics, it seems unlikely that she kept her distance from idolatry in the way expected of worshippers of God. Still, her sympathy with Judaism in its priestly form was a factor that Festus and his collaborators had not anticipated, and it weakened their position considerably. Indeed, it also inadvertently weakened the Roman position in Judea, in that it emboldened the already growing claim by priestly factions that they were the sole legitimate rulers of the Temple and its environs.

There was one significant consolation for Festus, Agrippa II, and Berenice: Poppaea decided she wanted to keep the high priest Ishmael with her in Rome, so another high priest needed to be appointed. Any enjoyment of that turn of events, however, was completely overshadowed by another. For reasons that the sources do not provide, Festus died in office.[6] As had happened so many times already, illness and death interrupted Herodian prospects in sudden, unpredictable ways – and this time the biological setback was quickly compounded by an escalating series of bad human decisions.

Nero dispatched Lucceius Albinus from a military position in Alexandria to take up the office of procurator of Judea. Albinus's background and career track were purely military, and his actions would reflect a lack of political acumen. At the same time, Agrippa II replaced the recently appointed Joseph Kabi with a new high priest, Ananus, who came from the most powerful of the high priestly families. Why Agrippa made this decision is unknown, although the prestige of Ananus's family extended back generations, and the appointment might have been intended to bring stability. It did not, and the decision proved fateful. Ananus's forebears included priests who had been involved in the death of Jesus. James, as Jesus's brother, was a natural target of Ananus's growing influence as well as of the animus of his family. In addition, James's widespread reputation in Jerusalem as a practitioner of the Nazirite vow as well as a sponsor of Nazirites (including Paul) made him a competitor to all other groups that desired to benefit from the prestige that came from association with the Temple. Ananus, in the interregnum between Festus's death and the arrival of Albinus, convened a session of the Sanhedrin and saw to the execution of James by stoning in the year 62.[7]

With this act a new ambition showed itself in the circle of Ananus. Once those of his party, known as the Sadducees, had believed it best for Rome to govern Judea directly in cooperation with the priesthood. After the death of Herod the Great, some of them had even appealed to Augustus not to install any of Herod's sons in his place, but to govern their region administratively as part of Syria.[8] Later, it had been Agrippa I's surprising achievement to seal the place of his kingship in the nexus between Rome and the Temple with priestly acceptance. Now, however, Ananus was acting apart from Agrippa II as well as in the absence of a Roman procurator.

In Josephus's description of events in his *Jewish Antiquities,* Ananus is arrogant and ruthless, and a typical Sadducee in that regard. Writing closer in time to the actions involved, however, the Josephus of the *Jewish War* made Ananus a noble, Periclean figure, eager only to protect the interests of the Temple and the priesthood.[9] The difference between those two portraits mirrors Josephus's rapid adaptation to the changing environments of Judea and of Rome. Born into a priestly family, Josephus aligned himself with what he thought at first was Ananus's militant but judicious insistence on the prerogatives of the priesthood. When that stance failed, he revised his opinion and his own stance drastically, becoming a supporter of the Roman campaign against Jewish militancy. The story of that transformation is woven into his narrative, and also, as will emerge, into his changing depiction of Berenice as he moved on from the *Jewish War* to write his *Jewish Antiquities.*

Although priestly militants praised Ananus, and Josephus held on to that partisanship in his first book only to give up his loyalty at a later stage, popular opinion in Jerusalem at the time of James's execution was divided. His identification with his brother's movement made James controversial, although his dedication to the Nazirite vow gave him the aura of consecration. His willingness to help introduce Paul into the Temple only complicated responses to James. Outrage at his execution, in effect a judicial murder, motivated a protest, which was brought to Albinus as the incoming procurator still made his way from Alexandria.[10] The complaint centered not only on the act of killing James, but also on the convening of the Sanhedrin without recourse to the Roman administration.

Albinus agreed with the protesters that Ananus should be deposed for his actions, and Agrippa II obliged, naming Jesus, son of Damneus, in his place. Predictably, the rapid turnover of high priests also inflamed feelings of animosity among priestly groups, but Albinus attempted to placate resistance by accepting the gifts and goodwill of the still influential Ananias, whose prestige rose in the city. Even Ananias, however, was not immune to the sicarii, who – despite Albinus's attempt to eliminate them – kidnapped some of Ananias's family's staff. When Albinus agreed to the release of some sicarii in exchange for the staff who had been kidnapped, he set in motion a cycle of hostage-taking familiar today in the experience of many states that have failed or are in the process of failing.[11]

By this stage it was apparent to Agrippa II that he needed to act openly on the Roman side in order to preserve his position. He achieved remarkable success in doing so. Reaching into his resources, he extended and improved his capital city at Caesarea Philippi, renaming it Neronias.[12] At the same time he saw to the construction of a theater in Beirut, a city outside his realm for which he had a particular affinity, and adorned it with statues. During this time, Berenice was also active in the field of patronage. The inscription at Athens discussed in the Introduction reflects a considerable donation, although of how much and for what purpose remain unknown. It is clear from the inscription that, contrary to what is sometimes asserted, Berenice was celebrated as a queen in the line of her father, Agrippa I, and not as the sister of Agrippa II.[13] Further, none of her three husbands is mentioned. She was portrayed as autonomously wealthy and influential, whatever the exact relationship with her brother might have been.

Although Agrippa II, and to a lesser extent Berenice, were able to burnish the perception of their standing in imperial relations by means of their patronage, their most pressing concern was their status on the ground in Jerusalem. Agrippa had changed the appointment of the high priest yet again, putting Jesus son of Gamaliel into office because he favored one faction over another.[14] Predictably, his actions further exacerbated factionalism. The greatest challenge to the Herodian position in Jerusalem, however, was that the vast project commenced in 20 BCE under Herod the Great to renovate and extend the Temple at last came to completion. Paradoxically, that epochal Herodian accomplishment came at a price, because the cessation of construction produced high unemployment, amounting to some eighteen thousand workers by Josephus's estimate.[15] Although Agrippa did authorize some additional paving work in Jerusalem, in comparison to his lavish project in Beirut, complete with the erection of idolatrous statues, the effort seemed jejune.

What was needed was a gesture from the Herodians that would express not only their regard and care for the Temple, but also their acknowledgment of the ruling force of the ancestral customs and laws of Judaism. Agrippa II never found that gesture, but Berenice did. Despite the increasingly difficult and violent culture surrounding worship in the Temple, she undertook to complete a Nazirite vow in Jerusalem. She was determined not merely to fund the vows of others, a well-established act of devotion among wealthy rulers and other donors, but also to appear herself as a Nazirite.

Berenice's resolve was complicated by yet another change of procurators. Gessius Florus, whose wife was a friend of Poppaea, now the wife of Nero, arrived to take Albinus's place. On his way out of office, Albinus had freely taken bribes in order to release prisoners.[16] The influx of criminals made it all the more expedient for Gessius Florus to engage in a policy of not pursuing armed gangs, provided they paid tribute to him. Josephus expressed the view that he forced war upon his Judean subjects.[17] Florus's policies of expropriation might have been encouraged by events in Rome, where Nero used the occasion of the great fire that broke out that year, in 64, to persecute Christians on a massive scale, and to reshape the city in his own image.[18] Gessius Florus was not specifically opposed to Christianity, but for some reason the friendship of his wife (named Cleopatra) with Poppaea did not translate into any high regard for Judaism. During this same period, Josephus gives an account of how he personally met with Poppaea in Rome during 63, seeking to have some priests who had been detained there released.[19] Her sympathies with Judaism, then, appear to have continued until the end of her life. But her sympathies have also been well described as eclectic, and clearly they were not sufficiently categorical to dissuade Gessius Florus from his exploitative practices, nor prevent him from behavior toward Berenice that became shameful.[20]

The queen completed her vow in Jerusalem after Gessius Florus had committed his greatest outrage to date in terms of the sensibilities of Judaism and the well-being of Jerusalem's population. In the process of adjudicating a dispute in Caesarea Maritima that arose when the extension of a synagogue was proposed, Gessius Florus had realized how much he could benefit from a variety of payoffs. He became increasingly cruel, both accepting bribes and doing nothing for those who had paid him. In his outright contempt for Jews and Judaism he was perhaps emboldened by the news in 65 that Poppaea had died in Rome; if Suetonius is to be believed, Nero had kicked her while she was pregnant and prompted her death.[21] Florus's appetite for gain grew, and any sense of restraint diminished: he confiscated seventeen talents from the Temple, an overt insult to its sanctity. This repeated a similar outrage just over thirty years earlier, during the time of Pontius Pilate, a much more peaceful period in Jerusalem, but bloodshed had nonetheless been the result then.[22] As in the case of Pilate, there were protests in the Temple, but Florus acted with much more cruelty than his predecessor. Pilate had ordered some of his troops to scatter the crowd gathered against him in the Temple with clubs; Florus marched cavalry and infantry to Jerusalem. He commandeered use of the Herodian palace, the residence of Agrippa II and Berenice in Jerusalem, from which he both ordered mass crucifixions and set his soldiers into the city in a program of looting.

Berenice, essentially sequestered in the same palace that Florus had commandeered, pursued her vow in the midst of the mounting violence. She sent some of her own officers, in place to protect her, to intercede with Florus, but to no avail. She even appeared before the procurator personally – barefoot, according to Josephus – to entreat his mercy.[23] In this way, she combined the powerful symbolism of the Nazirite vow, for which she shaved her head so that the consecrated hair could be offered in the Temple, and of penitence, in which shoes were commonly removed, as described in Mishnah Yoma 8:1. Her whole dramatic gesture was designed to convey her dedication to Judaic practice, so tracing her removal of footwear to an imitation of adepts of the Egyptian goddess Isis (as has been suggested) seems implausibly exoticizing.[24] In the midst of violence, at considerable personal risk, Berenice used nonviolent, ritual means grounded in Judaism to confront Florus with his unbridled behavior, while pursuing her own interests in implicitly encouraging him to withdraw from the Herodian palace. She acted, as always, for her family even as she courageously defended the sanctity of the Temple and associated structures by completing her vow of consecration.

Berenice's ritual vow and her peaceful confrontation with Gessius Florus did nothing to change the procurator's policy or conduct, but they did contribute to a growing sense of resistance within the city. Confronted by a new onslaught of forces sent by the procurator and designed to spread terror, a contingent of insurgents broke down the portico that permitted easy access to the Temple from the Roman garrison in the Antonia Fortress.[25] This move clearly frightened Florus, because he withdrew to Caesarea Maritima. For a moment, at least, he had deserted the field, leaving Berenice to fill the vacuum of power. She did just that, and with consummate skill. Berenice took the lead in composing and dispatching a letter of protest to the legate in Syria, detailing the outrages of Gessius Florus and appealing for his removal.[26] The procurator, naturally, had anticipated such complaints, and had himself appealed for military support. An officer was duly delegated by the Syrian legate to inquire into the situation, and the crucial meeting occurred outside Jerusalem, in the town of Yavneh.

Herodian representation at the meeting came not in the person of Berenice, but her brother. Agrippa II's intervention at this late stage was necessary, but his timing and his approach only encouraged aggressive attitudes from opponents such as Gessius Florus. During the months prior to the meeting, in 66, he had not been in Jerusalem, Tiberias, or Caesarea Philippi (now called Neronias). Instead, he had stayed in Alexandria, joining in the celebration of the new prefect of Egypt, a powerful position in a vital economic quadrant of the Roman Empire. The new prefect was none other than Tiberius Julius Alexander, the former procurator and the brother of Berenice's first husband. Maintaining that alliance had been crucial for the Herodians, but Agrippa's absence from Jerusalem during the pivotal events of 66 was scarcely helpful.[27] Had he been there with Berenice during the period of her vow, he might have moderated the procurator's behavior and perhaps have kept Gessius Florus from occupying the Herodian palace.

Whatever good Agrippa II was not able to do during his absence from Jerusalem, the actual harm he inflicted on the prospects of the city while at the conference in Yavneh was egregious. He sided with Gessius Florus against the resisters, and opposed the proposal to send a formal embassy to Nero in order to settle the matter definitively.[28] Josephus offers the explanation that by criticizing the resisters, Agrippa hoped to dissuade them from violent rebellion, but his actions from this point forward seem to be animated by a loyalty to Rome that had become a form of subservience.

When Agrippa II at last returns to Jerusalem in Josephus's account, it is to make a speech to a gathering in Jerusalem in which he articulates the position that Josephus himself came to defend: so great a power as Rome could not have emerged apart from God's will, thus resistance was a form of impiety against providence.[29] In Josephus's account, while Agrippa spoke he had his sister stand on the elevated platform of the Herodian palace, in clear view of his audience. At the close of the speech both he and his sister wept. In this case, Berenice's performance was in the interests of her brother's position more than her own, but it was no less affecting for that reason. Brother and sister showed how much they had learned from their father's capacity for display.

Agrippa II was a better courtier than any Herodian of his generation, but Berenice demonstrated finer instincts for public intervention. Had this final speech in Jerusalem proven effective, both could perhaps have claimed credit for the preservation of Jerusalem. In the hindsight of success, the positions of brother and sister might have been portrayed as complementary. Even so, as evidenced by his actions, Agrippa's priority was the imperial administration, while Berenice's priority was the sanctity of the Temple. It is not possible to know whether her approach of continued appeal against the actions of Gessius Florus would have been more effective, because she acceded to her brother's policy of siding with the procurator. In any case, Agrippa's plea for calm in Jerusalem lost all effectiveness when he explicitly called for the population to continue dealing with Gessius Florus and obey him. That proposal made Jerusalem unsafe for both Agrippa and Berenice, and they retreated to Neronias.[30] Their departure left the way clear for the takeover of Jerusalem by those bent on rebellion against Rome. The violence that had long been ambient in the city, and that had been mounting since the completion of construction in the Temple, now became a formal rupture between Jerusalem and Rome in 66.

The priestly administrator (*sagan*) of the Temple was named Eleazar, a son of Ananias. He took the opportunity offered him by the departures from Jerusalem of Gessius Florus, Agrippa II, and Berenice to declare that no gift from a gentile was to be accepted for sacrifice in the Temple – in effect asserting the autonomy of the priesthood from Rome's emperor. Agrippa sent cavalry in support of some in Jerusalem who opposed Eleazar, but they were defeated. Arson ravaged the Herodian palace in Jerusalem and the Antonia Fortress, destroying records of debt in the flames.[31] The city was no longer Roman or Herodian; instead it was riven by factional violence among various insurgent groups.

The events in Jerusalem triggered battles between gentiles and Jews not only in Judea and in Agrippa II's lands, but also in Syria and Egypt. The pattern became especially virulent in Alexandria, where Tiberius Julius Alexander sent in two legions, reinforced with two thousand troops from Libya, to quell Jewish rioters, killing fifty thousand people by Josephus's estimate.[32] His actions earned the prefect of Egypt the reputation of being an apostate from Judaism, but both Herodians and their in-laws clearly saw loyalty to Rome as so essential for Jewish survival that it was worth the death of some Jewish rebels. Survival of the whole had become the priority.

Agrippa II himself organized an army to march on Jerusalem with Cestius Gallus, the Syrian legate to whom Berenice had so recently appealed in regard to Gessius Florus. Even this combined force, however, did not prevail against the growing number of armed revolutionaries streaming into Jerusalem. The revolutionaries' confidence was such that a council assigned commanders of various regions. This was when Josephus, of proud priestly descent, took up the command of Galilee as an insurgent against Rome.[33] Hard experience would make him a convert to the ideology of providential Roman power. Yet even when writing his *Jewish War* a decade later, he recounted, in self-satisfied detail, his acumen in seeing to the defense of the cities assigned to him by the revolutionary council.

Agrippa II was a steady ally of Rome; indeed, his confidence in Roman arms sometimes caused him to make faulty tactical decisions. His city of Tiberias, for example, had been seized by rebels, and Agrippa might have intervened there in order to bring it back into his control. Instead he awaited the arrival of Roman cavalry, giving the rebels inside the city, aware of the impending battle, time to strengthen their opposition.[34] He never appeared to understand that enthusiasm on the part of his subjects for his Roman masters could be neither cajoled nor compelled. The Syrian legate's campaign from Antioch, with which Agrippa II had cooperated, had failed to retake Jerusalem, and Galilee had become a patchwork of factional fiefdoms. With so much of the region in revolt, only a massive intervention could restore Roman dominance. In the meantime, the Herodian palace in Tiberias was burned down, and Agrippa and Berenice saw much of their property and commercial ventures pillaged and destroyed.[35]

Later Roman historians describe the same period as perilous for the Roman Empire as a whole, because Nero engaged in some of his most scandalous behavior as war in Judea broke out and then raged. Grief for his dead wife Poppaea spurred his performative excesses with a slave boy named Sporus, whom he had had castrated and with whom he staged an elaborate wedding ceremony.[36] The emperor's reputation for narcissistic insanity would shortly bring an end to his reign and his life. Yet Nero clearly did appreciate that quelling the Judean revolt would require more than a reaction from locally available Roman forces, and that he needed a commander who could intervene massively across a large swath of territory.

Titus Flavius Vespasianus had served successfully in Roman Britain, as well as in political appointments. During a time when Nero was well aware of intrigue against him, too, Vespasian was a relatively loyal figure. From an equestrian family and approaching sixty years old, he posed less a threat to the emperor's position and his vanity than a more youthful general from an aristocratic family might have. Apparently the only complaint Nero had against Vespasian was that persistently, while in the imperial retinue during lyre concerts that the emperor gave in Greece, Vespasian sometimes absented himself or, if present, failed to pay attention to the point of falling asleep.[37] Wisely, Nero overlooked his pride on this occasion, and appointed Vespasian to retake Judea. His choice reversed the setback in Judea, and ultimately redeemed the prospects of the Roman Empire. Although Suetonius depicts Nero as debauched to the point of incompetence, his political and military judgment in this case proved to be astute.

The expedition directly under Vespasian's command, the fifth and the tenth legions, set out from Antioch, supported by Agrippa II's forces. At the same time, Vespasian's son Titus advanced from Alexandria with the fifteenth legion. The combined forces waged a campaign through Galilee that was especially bloody; villages, towns, and cities that did not surrender were destroyed, their surviving populations killed or sold into slavery. Josephus suggested that had all his orders been carried out, he might have resisted, or at least resisted better, the overwhelming onslaught of the Romans. But in fact, Josephus's military career once Vespasian's campaign was under way amounted to one long retreat. He fell back from one fortification to another: Sepphoris, Tiberias, and finally Jotapata. Hidden in a nearby cave after the city fell around him under Vespasian's brutal forty-seven day siege, Josephus later recounted having a dream that – by his priestly powers of interpretation – he knew to mean that "all fortune had passed to the Romans."[38] His companions were not at all ready to surrender alive, so Josephus put his trust in a system for drawing lots, to determine the order in which the soldiers would heroically slay one another rather than fall into Roman hands. The lots allegedly left only Josephus and one of his soldiers standing, and they both surrendered.

Josephus also recounts how he hailed both Vespasian and Titus as future Caesars during interviews after his capture. While such reports are self-serving, Tacitus also claims that a Judean prophecy had forecast the rise of the Flavian dynasty.[39] However much hindsight is involved in such claims, Josephus became an avid supporter of Vespasian and Titus, joining in propaganda for their cause and basically aligning himself with the position of Agrippa II. To a large extent, his newfound loyalties also involved substantial agreement with Berenice, of course, but he never accorded her the recognition and respect that he showed to her brother. Indeed, Berenice mostly drops out of Josephus's narrative at the point when she became one of the most famous (or notorious) women in the Roman Empire.

Josephus his did best to ingratiate himself with his new masters; likewise, Berenice and Agrippa II boldly welcomed both Vespasian and Titus. Unlike Josephus, however, the royal brother and sister did not need to prove their loyalty. They were Roman citizens of long standing from a line of client rulers, and a longer line of priestly genealogy; the loss of Jerusalem and then Tiberias was as much theirs as it was the Romans', and they had suffered the consequences of multiple setbacks more directly than anyone based in Rome. In the midst of the Galilean campaign, Vespasian and Titus accepted the invitation of Agrippa and Berenice to take twenty days of rest and recreation in Caesarea Philippi/Neronias.[40] From that time, the spring of 67, when she was thirty-nine years old and he twenty-seven, Berenice and Titus were in love, and their relationship would change not only their lives, but also the course of events in Judea and the Roman Empire as a whole. Josephus maintained a decorous silence about the relationship, an authorial policy designed to protect his Flavian protectors from rumor. To some extent, that approach also explains his increasingly ambivalent attitude toward Berenice.

Following that interlude, the families of Titus and Berenice behaved in a way that represented their mutual interests. Tiberias was restored to Herodian control, and Titus gave some of those captured to Agrippa II and Berenice to sell as slaves. Other Galilean cities were also taken, and at Gamla, Agrippa II himself was wounded in the elbow by a stone while taking part in the siege. Flavians and Herodians had made common cause.[41] They faced fierce opposition. In Gamla, five thousand people jumped to their deaths into the ravine below the city rather than surrender, and the Romans killed another four thousand people there.

By the spring of 68, victory for the Roman Empire, which could be sealed only by retaking Jerusalem, seemed within reach. At no point was the fighting easy; at this juncture Josephus refers to relentless "zealots" in control of the city. But the force of arms at the disposal of Vespasian and Titus was overwhelming. Vespasian in particular cleared the ground in the region around Jerusalem within Judea proper, while Titus remained as close as he could to Berenice in Galilee. By dealing with the considerable Galilean resistance, Titus further isolated Jerusalem, even as he offered security to his lover and her brother. In military terms, the deployment of the three legions under Vespasian and Titus, their coordination with the forces under Agrippa's control as well as those of other client rulers, and the movement of troops and cavalry over hundreds of miles had already been a considerable accomplishment, a stunning success, and a paragon of Roman military conquest in its remorseless violence.

As it turned out, the situation in Rome was less predictable than the battle for Judea. Nero was right to overlook Vespasian's inattentiveness during imperial performances, because other officials proved to pose more active threats. Chief among them was Galba, the legate in Hispania who seems, if Plutarch's description is followed without its special pleading, to have used the occasion of the revolt of his colleague in Gaul to accept acclamation as emperor.[42] Galba's rise to power was formalized by the Senate as Nero fled and then killed himself at the young age of thirty. Instability at the center of the Roman Empire would lead to four emperors coming to power in a single year. Berenice was a key figure in supporting the last of these four, who founded a new imperial dynasty in which Agrippa II and Berenice would receive glory and power by association.

CHAPTER SIX

Titus's Paramour in Rome

The military situation in Judea and Galilee had entered a decisive phase in terms favorable to Vespasian as well as to the Herodians. Titus was able to concentrate his energies as well as his affections in Galilee. Titus's passion, however, resulted in the eclipse of the role of Berenice in the writings of Josephus when he covered the period after she and Titus began their liaison. Josephus, after all, was writing under the patronage of the Flavian emperors, Vespasian at first and then Titus, followed by Domitian. When Titus became the princeps in 79 CE, that brought the end of his public relationship with Berenice. In agreement with Flavian policy Josephus does not even mention the beginning of their affair in 67, when Titus led his armies into Galilee and was hosted by Agrippa II and Berenice in Caesarea Philippi; Berenice and Titus are both present, but their relationship is unaccounted for in his narrative. In the *Jewish War,* he in effect turns Berenice into a non-person from the time she began her relationship with Titus.

Josephus's attitude toward her is all the more intriguing since he refers to Agrippa II in persistently cordial terms. The almost comic result of his bias, which surfaces brazenly in his *Jewish Antiquities,* is that he criticizes Berenice for alleged incest, but not her brother. He snipes at her in other ways, as well, contending that Drusilla married Felix only to flee Berenice's vengeful behavior, which was motivated by Drusilla's beauty.[1] As mentioned earlier, since Drusilla had already been married that is simply implausible, as is the assertion that Polemon married Berenice only because she was wealthy.

Fortunately for the task of historical assessment, Josephus's eclipsing of Berenice is partially compensated for in various ways. The time between Vespasian's rise and Titus's accession is just the interval in which Berenice catches the attention of Roman historians, and while they are no more inclined than Josephus to let her voice be present on the page, and are sometimes terse to the point of becoming cryptic – or chatty to the point of becoming "cattish," as Collingwood would say – they did leave behind indications of her activities.

Josephus also, in a much later work (his *Life*) lets slip his personal reasons for disliking Berenice, and in doing so inadvertently provides evidence of her influence and activity (as is discussed later). In addition, while recording the movements of Vespasian, Titus, and Agrippa II during the final years of the Judean war, Josephus provides us with occasions to see Berenice as a possible factor, even when she is not mentioned. That Judean war, the rise of the Flavian dynasty to power, Berenice's final foray into Roman politics, and her ultimate attempt to contribute to the success of the generational Herodian project all came to their denouement during the very period in which Josephus found reasons to ignore her. His refusal to mention Berenice and his motivations for that refusal, when uncovered, also point to how Berenice can be understood in her time and in her own terms.

Vespasian reacted with caution to the initial news regarding the challenge to Nero, and the report that provincial legates in Gaul and Hispania had raised forces in order to replace him. He knew well that there had been earlier conspiracies, most famously that of the popular senator Gaius Calpernius Piso in 65 CE, which had failed despite Piso's wide connections.[2] Now, three years later, Vespasian initially expected Nero to weather the storm, so he continued his deliberative campaign of taking Jerusalem by destroying sources of supply around the city. He was also aware, from the reports of deserters, that factional fighting inside Jerusalem had become deadly, and that living conditions there were atrocious. Yet he persistently resisted advice to advance immediately. He maintained a policy of encirclement and devastation well after he learned of the provincial coup against Nero, and that policy gave him room for political maneuvering.[3] His finely balanced response as a general revealed the shrewd qualities that would come to make him a successful emperor.

Camps were established, with the final assault in view, when news of Nero's death and Galba's acclamation reached Vespasian. He decided to pause his advance, dispatching Titus to Rome, accompanied by Agrippa II, in order to acknowledge the new ruler of Rome and to receive his orders concerning the campaign. Before their arrival in Rome, however, news came to Titus and Agrippa II of Galba's assassination in January 69, his replacement by Otho, and the contention with a third pretender, Vitellius, all of which is related by Tacitus.[4] Prior to his association with Galba, Otho had been legate in Lusitania, to which Nero had assigned him to clear the way for Nero's liaison with Otho's consort Poppaea.[5] Bad personal blood was clearly mingled with bad political blood. Because Vitellius commanded the armies in Germania, it is also evident that turmoil in European provinces was a major factor. The Roman Empire seemed at the mercy of provincial as well as personal grievance, with constant civil war in prospect.

Under what Josephus calls a "divine impulse," and what Tacitus refers to as a passion for Berenice, Titus returned to his father in Caesarea Maritima when he learned of Galba's death, while Agrippa II continued on to Rome.[6] Whatever motivated Titus, instability in Rome made it a problematic environment for the representation of Vespasian's interests at this stage. As a result Titus returned to his father at what proved to be the moment when the governance of the Roman Empire would be set out for the remainder of the first century CE. He also returned to the place where it would be settled, which was the Middle East rather than Rome. Tacitus indicates that Titus, apparently aware of the prospects that were opening up to his family, already thought in terms of his father becoming princeps, and had seen to a working alliance between Vespasian and Mucianus, the legate of Syria, toward this end.[7]

Just as Agrippa II had been absent from Jerusalem at a decisive moment, so also he was not in Caesarea Maritima when a decision was made that would profoundly affect the future of the Roman Empire. As we observed, even as Vespasian learned of increasing chaos in Rome, he maintained his former war tactics, pursuing the encirclement of Jerusalem. But with Otho's death in April 69 during a campaign against Vitellius, it was obvious that, while the issue of Judea and Jerusalem had been all but settled, the prospects for Rome were in very serious doubt. News of Vitellius's predations in the imperial city made Vespasian decide not to acknowledge him as emperor, as he had been prepared to do in the case of Galba, but instead to try for the prize himself.[8]

The thought process that led Vespasian to seek being acclaimed emperor himself is clearly set out by Josephus, although the narrative surrounding how that argument came to be articulated is unconvincing. Josephus pictures a reluctant Vespasian persuaded to supplant Vitellius by unnamed "officers and soldiers." Their speech is not attributed to any specific individuals, but it touches on crucial factors that would in fact make for Vespasian's success: his armies had been more successful in Judea and Galilee than Vitellius's forces had been in Germania, he was more virtuous and deserving of rule than Vitellius, Titus with his younger brother Domitian was ready to support Vespasian and eventually to replace him while Vitellius was childless – and three full legions were at Vespasian's disposal, together with the troops supplied by client kings such as Agrippa II.[9]

There is nothing wrong about this argument, and in fact Vespasian would follow out its line of reasoning so thoroughly that it does not seem he was unprepared for it; Tacitus depicts a very active, engaged Vespasian at this stage.[10] But it is unlikely that "officers and soldiers" would articulate this kind of detailed case, animated not only by a lucid diagnosis of conditions on the ground in Europe as well as Judea, but also by a willingness to change the very basis on which Rome was ruled. According to this account, these nameless military advisers pressed for Vespasian's acclamation with the vigorous confidence that Titus could then seamlessly succeed him. In the chaotic conditions of the time, the model of monarchy had an appeal, since biological succession offered the prospect of relative stability. But the Roman Republic had emerged in the overthrow of a king, and however dictatorial the rulers from the time of Julius Caesar and his adoptive son Augustus had been, Rome generally skirted strictly hereditary kingship. Tacitus, in fact, attributes to Galba the view that even Augustus had been too bound by family considerations in making Tiberius his successor, while Galba claimed to search throughout the entire *re publica* for a suitable successor.[11] A reversal of that calculated policy, to embrace hereditary succession, represented a decision that was only Vespasian's to make. That he did so is a sign of the volatility of the "Year of the Four Emperors," and his own calculated audacity. Although Josephus implausibly attributes to Vespasian's soldiers the initiative to promote the monarchic model, the general's consultation was indeed very wide, ultimately including an astrologer.[12] His approach – a combination of careful preparation and decisive intervention – was the fruit of his success as a military commander and would prove to be key to his emergence as a transformational emperor.

By this point in the *Jewish War*, Josephus has laid the ground for the claim that the monarchic proposal came spontaneously from the army by means of a long digression – one in which he details the overwhelming successes of the Roman military, depicted as the engine of their empire.[13] This is the army that his prophetic revelation while he was under siege at Jotapata had disclosed to be the instrument of providence; here in the allegedly anonymous advice to Vespasian, Josephus gives it a speaking role. The content of the argument, however, together with Vespasian's conduct once he resolved to act in accordance with its logic, shows where its influences lie. Vespasian was not isolated in any colloquy he may or may not have had with his troops. Titus had personally returned from his abortive mission to Rome; later in the narrative, when Vespasian goes into action, the collaboration with the Syrian legate Mucianus also proves pivotal, and periodic consultation in person and through emissaries was necessary to effect that. Agrippa II was still in Rome, but Berenice was likely present with Titus in what was clearly a council of conquest that Vespasian had convened, accompanied but not guided by a casual discussion in the barracks.

The probability of Berenice's presence resides not only in Titus's return from the abortive mission to Rome, but also in the quality of the argument made for Vespasian to act. Writing at a later time, but with no visible sympathy for Berenice, Tacitus observes that she used her wealth and influence to see to Vespasian's advance, portraying both Berenice and her brother as supporters, and gratuitously referring to her still youthful beauty.[14] Her wealth alone would have recommended her to Vespasian, who had had difficulty raising loans even from his brother Sabinus in Rome.[15] Josephus also describes Agrippa II as rushing back from Rome when informed of the plans that were developing: those plans came into focus with Berenice's active and attractive encouragement before Agrippa was on the scene. Her Herodian influence helps account for the innovative embrace of the hereditary succession of a monarchy, and for the emphasis on the place of Titus within the imperial plans from the outset, as well for Josephus's mention of the importance of royal Herodian troops within the argument of the "officers and soldiers."

Vespasian went into action in a way that betrays his continuing reliance on connections that Berenice facilitated. Here again, Josephus has the reluctant general pressed into action by his soldiers – now with their swords drawn, no less – but Vespasian acts so decisively as to subvert any sense of his reluctance.[16] His explicitly "first" object was to secure the backing of Alexandria, because he knew that its resources of wheat would enable him to supply Rome and, if necessary, control the flow of provisions so as to starve Vitellius out.[17] He also wanted the support of the legions serving under Tiberius Julius Alexander in Egypt, and wrote a letter to the influential prefect. Berenice's one-time brother-in-law responded by having both soldiers and civilians swear an oath of allegiance to Vespasian, a response that evidently needed more preparation than a bare letter to eventuate.[18] That oath, given on the first of July in 69, was commemorated as the first day of Vespasian's principate.[19] As Tacitus indicated, Berenice's influence was critical, because Egypt was vital to the success of any coup. For the coup in the capital itself, Vespasian delegated Mucianus and another general, Antonius Primus, to engage Rome and its environs, not least to release his son Domitian from custody in the city. Although the conquest of Rome happened more rapidly than the capture of Jerusalem, it was far from bloodless.

As Vespasian knew, the challenge of staying in power was greater than that of seizing power. He had recourse to far more military resources than Galba, Otho, and Vitellius could ever command. Their failed efforts had made him the fourth new emperor of that chaotic year, but he aspired to be the final and definitive aspirant of the series, and to found an actual dynasty. That ambition required plentiful assets for the repair of Rome as well as a redoubtable campaign of propaganda in order to project the allegedly overwhelming power of the new regime. While Mucianus established Domitian as the temporary ruler of Rome, Vespasian stayed in Alexandria with Tiberius Julius Alexander organizing relief for Rome and gathering resources for the new Flavian order in Rome. That done, he headed for the city, but not before dispatching Titus to complete the siege of Jerusalem and finish the war in Judea, assigning Tiberius Julius Alexander to take up command of troops from the Euphrates as well as Alexandria. In noting this assignment, which effectively made Tiberius second in command to Titus, Josephus describes Tiberius Julius Alexander as the young Flavian's most trusted friend and preeminent among his counselors during the entire period of the war, largely because he had supported the dynasty when its prospects were far from certain.[20] This characterization reflects the formative role that Tiberius Julius Alexander played in shaping the Flavian dynasty.

Berenice receives no notice from Josephus in his account of this period, yet her connection with Alexandria and her partisanship of

Herodian monarchy, as well as her intimacy with Titus, all contributed to the Flavian project, which redefined the role of the princeps and his son with terms and resources that came from Egypt and Judea. When Vespasian connected his rise to alleged prophecies by omen and ancient sources of a ruler from the east, he was making an astute political observation as well as letting fly a gambit of propaganda that echoed in several quarters.[21] That it was propaganda is implicit in Tacitus's laconic remark that the oracles of Vespasian's success were believed only after he came to power. Dio Cassius, on the other hand, approvingly quotes Josephus's embrace of Vespasian as Rome's providential ruler.

For the propaganda to be effective, victory in Judea was evidently essential, and that was the responsibility of Titus once Vespasian had departed for Rome. Chaos during the Roman transition, complicated by the arrogant behavior of Domitian and a severe shortage of grain, demanded the emperor's presence.[22] Titus knew that efficiency in capturing Jerusalem was essential for securing acclaim in Rome.[23] Josephus describes the situation inside and outside Jerusalem in detail, with particular emphasis on Titus's courage and effectiveness, flatteringly calling him "Caesar," and vaunting his own utility as a propagandist as he shouted out to people on the walls to surrender.[24] By his own account, Josephus declaimed a litany of Roman conquests of epic proportion, designed to show that those besieged were warring against the inevitable, and therefore against God, as well as against Rome. During one of these harangues, a stone knocked him unconscious.[25] This treatment at the hands of the besieged was not surprising. Not only was he a traitor to his own stated position at the beginning of the war; he was also making the manifestly untrue claim that Titus wished to extend clemency to Jerusalem. Titus himself undermined Josephus's position by his policy of crucifying hundreds of people who escaped the city in order to forage.[26] Within the city, the still internecine fighting among sicarii, Zealots, Idumean bands, and priestly factions compounded the results of a famine so severely that cannibalism was the result.

Despite chronicling the grisly details of the inexorable Roman campaign, Josephus goes out of his way, however implausibly, to stress that Titus urged the surrender of the city so the Temple could be spared. He depicts the conquering general as moved at the sight of suffering in a way that the rebel leaders were not.[27] Convinced that God was on his side, he wished to spare the Temple, but the resisters used it as their redoubt. When sacrifices ceased, Titus ordered Josephus to translate and announce his offer that battle should be waged away from the Temple, already threatened with fire, so that sacrifices could continue.[28] Even Roman soldiers held the Temple in greater esteem than the revolutionaries in Josephus's depiction, and Titus himself comes to voice his vociferous support, vowing to preserve the Temple despite the rebels' profanation, which Josephus blamed for the loss of divine protection. In Josephus's telling, the fighting included arson on both sides, but especially on that of the Jews. Only after the rebels set fire to porticos connecting the Antonia to the Temple did Titus order the gates of the Temple to be set alight.[29]

Whatever Titus's exact intentions were, from this point on events overtook him – even in Josephus's description. The fire set by his troops spread, and his orders to extinguish the blaze were not entirely carried out. Titus's resolve in Josephus's account was nonetheless that the Temple should remain, a decision he made in a council of his senior officers, headed by Tiberius Julius Alexander, who is described at this point as the prefect of all the forces. A contingent sent to follow through on the order to put out the fire met resistance, however, and a soldier, "by divine impulse" and without any order, threw a burning brand into the complex around the Sanctuary. In Josephus's conception, some actions were animated by intentions that went beyond human motives. "Divine impulse" had brought Titus back to Berenice in time to plan the accession of Vespasian as princeps, and now a nameless soldier lit the fire that was God's just judgment. Bedlam ensued, as soldiers engaged resisters amidst the flames. Supposedly against Caesar's will, and despite the intervention of his officers, the Temple burned.[30]

The plunder that followed showed no sign of restraint. Yet Titus, in a speech attributed to him by Josephus during the announcement of terms, claims that he and his father conducted themselves with reserve, and that he had acted on behalf of the Temple, to which the resisters had set fire with their own hands. His demand for surrender was not accepted; fighting resumed, fires multiplied. Although he declared that he had triumphed with God's help in taking such a city by the end of September in 70, it was in ashes. Of the survivors, some were killed, some were reserved for a triumph in Rome, some were sold into slavery, and some were kept for gladiatorial games. Josephus estimates the number of prisoners taken during the war at just under 100,000, and the dead during the siege of Jerusalem at over one million.[31]

Titus delivered the victory that his father had prepared, and proceeded to rule Jerusalem as a military conquest. Although celebration and self-congratulation began there and then, Titus quickly made his way first to Caesarea Maritima, and then to Caesarea Philippi, where he stayed longest and saw to spectacles. Prisoners were tossed to wild animals, or organized in groups to do combat with one another.[32] Although Berenice and Agrippa II would have been present for these games, Josephus does not mention them. Josephus's silence in their regard, and his extravagant characterization of Titus's attitude toward the Temple, both demand attention, and the two issues are connected.

Josephus wrote his *Jewish War* for distribution in 75, the same year that Dio Cassius indicates that the Temple of Peace was dedicated in Rome. By then Titus had returned to Rome, joining his father Vespasian, with Titus's brother Domitian in a subsidiary role, in a triumph that was later commemorated in the Arch of Titus as it stands today – which prominently depicts captured implements from the Temple in Jerusalem. Josephus describes the triumph in detail: those sacred objects, the splendor of other spoils as they were paraded, the procession of exotic animals, the prisoners on exhibit, the floats depicting battles and burning buildings, the display of actual ships, and the public jubilation at the executions that climaxed the proceedings.[33] He leaves no doubt about his own function as a Flavian apologist. Once known in Aramaic as Yosef bar Mattityahu, he more than merited his eventual designation as Flavius Josephus in library catalogs around the world.

Within that apologetic purpose, silence in regard to Berenice was natural, because Vespasian and Titus had not yet determined how best to deal with the question of acknowledging Titus's relationship with her. With the deposition of some of the sacred implements of the Temple in Jerusalem within the Temple of Peace, they also implicitly raised another, more fateful issue: whether Jerusalem might again see its own Temple rebuilt. In both regards, Josephus stayed true to the Flavian position at that time in keeping his own counsel. But in a few years the ground shifted under his feet.

Berenice had been neither silent nor inactive in the period after Vespasian's accession, whatever impression Josephus might have liked to give. She had played a role in that remarkable ascent to power, and welcomed the victorious Titus back to Caesarea Philippi, where their relationship had begun. In fact, writing at a much later period, Josephus inadvertently reveals that she continued to be influential there in matters of policy. In his *Life*, Josephus complains bitterly about a rival during the early days of the war, Justus of Tiberias.[34] Justus and Josephus, long after the events, engaged in a controversy concerning which of them had been responsible for the defection of Tiberias from Agrippa II during the revolt and the city's consequent attack on its neighbors.

As part of his argument, Josephus twice remarks that Agrippa II, authorized by Vespasian, had every right and reason to have Justus put to death, but that Berenice's intercession resulted in a sentence of imprisonment instead. In these representations, Agrippa II wields the power to adjudicate, and Berenice influences that adjudication. It is also of interest that Josephus refers in the *Life* to Berenice's ownership of stores of wheat. He wrote this short book near the year 100, providing an appendix to *Jewish Antiquities* as part of a pamphlet war with Justus. By then it appears that Agrippa II had died.[35] Berenice might have also died by this point, too, but Josephus continues to complain about her in a way that suggests otherwise.

Complaints about Berenice's influence in the administration of justice predate Josephus's last book. His contemporary Quintilian's remark that he pleaded a case in Rome before her has caused puzzlement, but makes sense if she participated in an imperial council at Vespasian's wish, which may well have happened.[36] She had after all served with Agrippa II on a *consilium* that guided Porcius Festus in his disposition of the case involving Paul of Tarsus, and Quintilian shows awareness of her influence in Rome in a similar way. Her knowledge would have been of great use in the many disputes that arose in Judea as a result of the war. In addition, her wealth resulted in her having a literally vested interest in many of the suits presented for adjudication. So when Quintilian comments that he once spoke on behalf of Queen Berenice before the person herself, that is notable but not really odd. Issues of property in the ravaged conditions of Judea, Samaria, Galilee, and Gaulanitis were bound to involve Herodian ownership or claims of ownership.

Berenice's influential presence in Rome is also clearly signaled by Dio Cassius. He reports that both Agrippa II and Berenice arrived in Rome in 75. Agrippa was then awarded the *ornamenta praetoria,* a symbolic honor but also for him a sentimentally meaningful one, since his father had been accorded that under Gaius.[37] Berenice moved into the imperial palace, and Dio Cassius complains that, having been promised marriage, Berenice was already behaving as Titus's wife. In a reversal of her previous relationship to Agrippa II in terms of power, she ostentatiously displayed her influence while he saw to practical governance in his now devastated territories. Geographically, however, as ever she remained at the hub of the realm (Caesarea Philippi, and then Rome), while her male counterpart traveled. That provides a suitable time period for her appearance within a Roman *consilium* of the kind that Quintilian describes.

Considerable discussion has surrounded the relative delay in Berenice's arrival after the celebratory triumph for Vespasian and Titus. But the timing coincided, in Dio Cassius's account, with the decision to honor Agrippa II and to inaugurate the Temple of Peace. Vespasian, Titus, and later Domitian all issued coinage on the theme *Judaea Capta,* but at this time in 75 a new attitude was tested. Indeed, Dio Cassius refers to Berenice as being "at the height of her power;" she was far from a symbol of defeat, but instead was consort of the emperor-to-be. Berenice's relationship with Titus was not new, but as it matured it manifested itself with increasing confidence. Indeed, the couple's willingness for their relationship to become known stands in sharp contrast with the silence of Josephus regarding Berenice in *The Jewish War.*

Criticism of their partnership, however, became severe, particularly among Cynic critics. One, named Diogenes, entered a full theater and indulged in a long harangue against Titus and Berenice. He was flogged as a result of his performance. Another, named Heras, pressed the same criticism in public, and was beheaded for his trouble. The harsh treatment was to some extent precedented by the memory, recorded by Dio Cassius, of a senator named Helvidius Priscus who had resisted the idea of Titus's succession of Vespasian, a basic trait of monarchy. Vespasian reacted by having Helvidius Priscus executed. Titus, too, was quite willing and able to defend himself. Since he was prefect of the Praetorian Guard, the execution of justice often fell in his hands; conflicts of interest did not disturb him. His increasingly visible power, and his willingness to use it ruthlessly, coincided with Berenice's increasing visibility as his consort.

The Cynics' long speeches, to which Titus reacted violently, especially in the case of Heras, might have given the first public airing to the charge that Berenice and Agrippa II had long been committing incest. Added to the charge that Titus's liaison with Berenice was making him vulnerable to the control of a defeated enemy, the complaint would account for the groundswell of opposition that Titus resisted, and yet in the end could not ignore. For the time being, however, the treatment of Diogenes and Heras shows where Titus's loyalties lay. The timing of their complaints also suggests that prior to 75, Berenice had indeed been parted from Titus since he left for his triumph in Rome.[38] Had she processed with him, first in the Middle East and then in Rome, criticism would evidently have come sooner.

Although Josephus would later turn against Berenice, and endorse criticism along the Cynics' lines, in the second half of the 70s CE he shared with her the hope that the Temple, destroyed more as a result of the predations of the Herodians' Jewish enemies than by the Romans (in Josephus's opinion as well as hers), might yet be restored. There was a precedent, after all: the Persian emperor Cyrus had permitted the Second Temple to be built on the ruins of Solomon's Temple, which the Babylonians had destroyed in 587 BCE, and Herod the Great had eventually made this second, replacement Temple into the greatest religious edifice that Judaism had ever seen, or would see in its history. In the midst of recounting the campaign of Titus, Josephus provides a detailed description of the Temple that was about to be destroyed. The portrayal may seem digressive, but in his mind the Temple and the Roman army were the twin institutions of divine providence, both of which Josephus had made it his goal to serve.

Indeed, prior to this description of the Temple Josephus voices the hope, a bold one to articulate in 75, that a return to the Sanctuary's former glory might yet be possible.[39] What he says out loud had its best prospect of success if Berenice could succeed in not only living as Titus's wife, but also joining with Titus in a recognized marriage. On this topic Josephus's silence reflects Flavian policy in the period when he wrote *The Jewish War.* At the same time, his tortured account of Titus's personal attitude toward the Temple, thoroughly implausible as history, reflects the Flavians' self-portrayal as beneficent conquerors as well as Josephus's attempt to shape Flavian policy by appealing to the themes of their own reckonings of their virtues. The Temple vessels carefully deposited in the Temple of Peace and in the imperial palace itself could easily have served in a restored Temple in Jerusalem, protected again by a Herodian client-king.[40] In addition, with Berenice in Rome as Titus's wife,

Agrippa II might have inherited the full territory and authority of his father, realizing the ambitions of Herod the Great.

All such hopes, as well as the prospects of the Flavian dynasty, were compromised by Titus's behavior, which became ruthless and violent. He had reacted viciously when Berenice was criticized by Cynics of various kinds, and became even more ferocious when one of his father's former supporters turned against him. Suetonius reports that Aulus Caecina Alienus was caught mounting a coup against Vespasian, and this seems to be the motivation for Titus's bloody treatment of him. But his reaction is so violent that it seems likely, as indicated in the later *Epitome de Caesaribus,* that Titus acted in response to another assault on Berenice's reputation.[41] Using his authority as prefect of the Praetorian Guard, Titus invited Caecina to dinner, then had him knifed when he was leaving the feast. As a symbol of his own power and Berenice's influence, the act provoked fear, but also triggered opposition at a more serious level than he had encountered before.

On this occasion, the ordinarily indulgent Vespasian did not condone or overlook his son's rashness; Titus already had a reputation of cruelty, but this barely disguised judicial killing provoked objections in the Senate. Some gesture was necessary to show that Titus intended to reform. Ending his public relationship with Berenice was the obvious way forward. When Suetonius writes that Titus immediately had Berenice depart from Rome, both he and she are described as reluctant to part with one another. E. Mary Smallwood, in an acute comment that recapitulates an observation of the playwright Jean Racine in the seventeenth century, called attention to Suetonius's phrasing.[42] Racine describes Titus as *invitus,* unwilling to end the relationship. The same term is used by Aeneas in Vergil's *Aeneid* when he speaks of how he left Dido. If that allusion is understood, the depiction would accord with Suetonius's portrayal of Titus as becoming a better Roman once the break from Berenice (and other alleged indulgences) was effected. But Suetonius also depicts Berenice as unwilling (*invitam*), as if she also took part in the difficult decision. They both grieved the prospect of a painful separation. Both also should have regretted the consequences of what they had provoked with their public posturing, whether violent (in Titus's case) or performative (in Berenice's case).

Reaction against Titus and Berenice, provoked by their behavior, threatened the couple's relationship, Berenice's ambition as a Herodian, hopes of restoring the Temple in Jerusalem, and even Titus's accession to the principate. But the gesture of separation from Berenice was effective, and served as the germ of the imperial propaganda that Titus had reformed from being a profligate heir to growing into a model of a self-denying emperor. Suetonius would even depict Titus's change as involving giving up young men as well as Berenice.[43] The depiction seems part of a deliberate comparison of the young Titus with Nero. But in 79 there was every reason for Titus and Berenice to hope that, parted against their will, they might be able one day to live together again, and perhaps even marry after time, relative calm, and propaganda could exercise their effects. Vespasian, after all, was still vigorous, despite his tendency to suffer gout, and might eventually allow his son some leeway.

A series of crises, however, extended Berenice's stay away from Rome. In the midst of a characteristically full schedule, Vespasian fell ill with an intestinal complaint, and as he attempted to recover at his villa in Cutiliae, the infection took his life.[44] Titus, thrust into the role of princeps, was in no position to bring Berenice back to Rome, especially because his energies were taken up by two epic disasters in the city. The first of these was the eruption of Vesuvius, and its destruction of Pompeii, also in 79. Wherever Berenice was staying, near or far from Rome, she would have learned of the death there of her sister Drusilla and Drusilla's son, named Agrippa.[45] Nature itself must have seemed to be conspiring against the Herodians.

The second disaster compounding Titus's troubles was the outbreak of yet another fire in Rome. Many landmarks of the city, especially temples, and structures representing much of the investment his father had put into construction (derived in large measure from his seizure of wealth from Jerusalem and its Temple), were wiped out in the conflagration. Titus saw to repairs while he continued work on the huge amphitheater, today called the Colosseum, which his father had begun. His energy at this point appeared inexhaustible, and was no doubt buoyed by a visit from Berenice that Dio Cassius mentions.[46] She could come to salute the new emperor as a matter of state, while keeping her distance as a matter of politics. Even while dealing with the crises, Titus also sponsored many spectacles, continuing a habit he had enjoyed in Caesarea Philippi. He was very much himself: dynamic, if a bit overweight, and whatever Suetonius indicated, still dedicated to fulfilling his own pleasures. At the age of forty-one, however, Titus contracted a fever and retreated to his dead father's villa in Cutiliae. He died there himself in 81.[47] With his death the dream of reviving the Temple in Jerusalem under Herodian rule in Judea came to an abrupt end, along with Berenice's imperial prospects.

Epilogue

Domitian, Vespasian's younger son, immediately assumed his dead brother's office. His takeover was so rapid that Suetonius reported on conjectures that Domitian had conspired to have Titus killed, had hastened his death, or at least had put his succession into action before Titus had actually died.[1] Suetonius was representative of the aristocracy in his antipathy toward Domitian; his generally successful principate came at the cost of curtailing already reduced senatorial powers. It was he who brought to completion ambitious Flavian building projects, adding top and bottom tiers to the Colosseum and consolidating the imperial palace; centralized finances so as to stabilize the economic basis of governance; and insisted on a return to traditional religious ways. That success involved raising taxes, burnishing the claim of the gods' backing of the princeps by declaring his predecessor divine, tightening control over newly appeared "superstitions" such as Christianity, and turning away from his father's, and especially his brother's, philo-Judaism.

In Asia Minor the Revelation to John, the last book in the New

Testament, compared Domitian to Nero, "the beast" of popular imagination. Although the language of the Apocalypse is dense and violent, it targets the issues of Domitian's attempt to regulate the production of grain and wine, along with his stringent policies of taxation.[2] In the minds of early Christians, the call to martyrdom involved economic oppression, not only immediate threats to life. The more he centralized administration and emphasized traditional Roman religion, the more Domitian alienated fringe religions within the empire. Nearer to home, aristocratic opposition in the Senate and resistance to his brutality within his own entourage compounded inveterate doubts about hereditary rule; the result was a coup against Domitian and his assassination by members of his own court in 96.[3]

Domitian was nonetheless the longest ruling Flavian, a longevity that meant that his policies put an end, for a time, to Jewish hopes for the restoration of the Temple. During the same period, Herodian hopes for rule in Judea and Jerusalem were also set aside. Even historians such as Suetonius, although critical of Domitian and a great supporter of Titus, simply wrote off Berenice as a wicked influence. Suetonius claimed that people feared Titus would become a new Nero: reckless in sexual escapades, in which Berenice featured as the apex, and someone who knew no restraint in his self-indulgence.[4] This characterization classifies her as one among many profligate connections, including homosexual liaisons – that is, well below the status afforded her by later historians who compared her to Cleopatra. Suetonius's portrayal was far from original, comparable to what Tacitus wrote earlier about Titus's passion for Berenice and what Dio Cassius noted later about her assuming the rights of a wife, with all of them perhaps encouraged by the accusations of Titus's Cynic critics.[5] Suetonius even portrays Titus's promise to marry Berenice as an example of his excess. Exercises in *damnatio memoriae* are prone to aggregating accusations and complaints, whether or not they are commensurate with one another.

Josephus also fell in with the literary fashion of denigrating Berenice. The change in his attitude toward her is striking. Writing his *Jewish War,* to be released in 75, the same year that Berenice arrived in Rome, he stayed silent about her when narrating events from the time Titus arrived in Galilee. That nonetheless permitted Josephus to depict Berenice's heroism in confronting Gessius Florus and her devotion to the Temple in 66. Those familiar with the *Jewish War* would know Berenice as a local Judean heroine who recognized the authority of Rome in Jerusalem, not as the mistress of Titus. Similarly, Josephus's portrait of Titus as unwilling to see the Temple destroyed flattered the emperor-to-be for his restraint, and offered the hope that the Temple might be built again.

In his *Jewish Antiquities*, in contrast, distributed during the winter of 93–94 when Domitian was still firmly in power, Josephus spread the rumor of Berenice's incest, and relished describing her defects of character – even accusing her of bullying Drusilla out of jealousy for her younger sister's beauty. Jealousy for the beauty of a relative, interestingly, was one of Dio Cassius's charges against the notorious Messalina, and reflects a standard rhetoric of misogyny.[6] By the time Josephus wrote his *Life,* he was going to the extreme of impugning Berenice's loyalty to Rome in view of her support of Justus of Tiberias, himself an exemplar of treachery in Josephus's self-justifying depiction.[7] Since the *Life* was produced under Nerva or Trajan, Josephus's attitude seems strangely vindictive, considering Berenice was no longer an influence in the imperial court.

When Berenice and her brother died is not precisely known, but it would be surprising if Josephus continued his campaign of vilification if she were dead by the time he wrote the *Jewish Antiquities,* as is sometimes surmised. It seems likely that the funeral for her former lover in 81 would have led both Agrippa II and Berenice to be in Rome then, but that is not known; similarly, their return to Caesarea Philippi afterward, and their eventual deaths there, are matters of inference, reasonable though the inferences seem to be in this case. Josephus never returned to his native land, even though the quality of writing in his *Life* suggests that his secretarial support in Rome was waning. Perhaps his attitude toward Berenice was shaped by a refusal on her part to offer Josephus any of the patronage that he craved as well as required. His charge of incest would then have had a personal motivation. Once the claim is present, attempts to adjudicate it are natural. Grace Harriet Macurdy, who did more than any other single scholar to put the study of Berenice on a critical footing, expressly criticizes historians who accept the assertion.[8] Juvenal's sixth satire is, after all, a satire.

That Berenice does not come to voice in the same sources that depict her actions as influential is a persistent frustration today, one grounded in the awareness that her intentions mattered within the events of her time. That sense was not, of course, shared by the ancient sources that refer to her, and some modern writers have provided an imaginative leap to provide what those sources withheld. During the seventeenth century, Madeleine de Scudéry was the author of a collection of letters allegedly written by ancient women and designed for the salon culture of her time. In this collection, she wrote a sensitive meditation on the relationship between love and the ambition for power under the cover of a letter from Berenice to Titus.[9] As the title of the work intimates by referring to her brother as the author, Madeleine de Scudéry negotiated complicated terrain. Her book takes the perspective of a series of women from antiquity, and pursues their identities as a project for her own time.

Two of Scudéry's emphases are particularly telling, and reflect her desire to elucidate the sources, even as she shapes them to her ends. The first is Berenice's confidence in Titus's love for her, to the point of writing that, were the decision entirely his, Titus "would prefer possession of Berenice over the empire of all the world."[10] The force of the Roman state, however, the second emphasis in the person of the commanding figure Vespasian, compels Titus to act as he does. The power of a heroic inheritance is also claimed by Berenice, so much so that she admits that others think ambition is for her a greater motivation than love. But she protests that love is her driving force: she encourages Titus to take up the power that is coming to him, and even to share it with another woman, while appealing to him never to "share the heart where you made me reign." For Berenice, Titus's heart is empire enough, and in a postscript Scudéry remarks that Berenice was indeed Titus's "last passion" since he died so soon after her departure from his court.

Scudéry writes often in the letter of the violence involved with governing, and yet does not acknowledge that Titus had used the powers available to him in Rome to deal cruelly with those who opposed and insulted Berenice. The strong distinction between the empire of the world and the empire of the heart, too, which is Scudéry's theme, was not likely featured in the reflection of any member of the Herodian dynasty. But such criticisms do not diminish the analytic acuity of Scudéry's search for the human intent within Berenice's complex actions, and the identification of that intent as passionate is vital to any understanding of what she did.

The most influential work on Berenice from the seventeenth century, and the single most important contribution during the modern period as a whole, is Jean Racine's tragedy from 1670, *Bérénice*. In it, Racine shows the influence not only of Madeleine de Scudéry, but also of Jean Regnault Segrais and Pierre Le Moyne. More prominently, *Bérénice* was in active competition with Pierre Corneille's

Tite et Bérénice, which opened just a week after Racine's play premiered.[11] Clearly, Berenice had already built an audience for Racine; just as clearly, Racine's sublimation of all the action implied in the tale to the relationship that Berenice has with Titus produces a concentrated simplicity. The Aristotelian unities of time, place, and plot are distilled further, within the intricacy of a mature love between the characters depicted in a way that produces a tragedy but without a death.

The intensity of Racine's writing, a masterful example of the French alexandrine, coordinates language and emotion. At the play's close, Bérénice advises her ardent but disappointed lover Antiochus, who is also Titus's intimate friend, that he needs to resign himself to the stark fact of her love for Titus, and Titus's love for her; "Frame your conduct to Titus's and mine: I love him, I flee him; Titus loves me, he leaves me."[12] Her disciplined intensity contrasts with the bumbling attempt of Titus to tell Bérénice earlier in the play that they must part. Because he cannot bring himself to speech, the syllables of lines are made up by coordinating his breaks with Bérénice's interjections, until Titus simply withdraws.[13] The presentation establishes Bérénice as the principal character in the scene, a feature mirrored at the close of the play.

Since Titus reveals his decision to have Bérénice depart before he has any interaction with her, on the grounds of opposition to her in Rome as well as in Roman law, some critics have doubted his real feelings for her. Yet Titus acknowledges that his intent had been to bring Bérénice with him to the pinnacle of power, and declares that only the death of his father made him realize that he needed to renounce himself, which necessarily involves renouncing her.[14] As the play progresses, Titus discloses the depth of his attachment to Bérénice, not only in direct expressions of love, but also in a personal disclosure to his friend Antiochus that although his heart cannot act contrary to Rome's will, Bérénice remains his unique desire.[15] In an unexpected admission to himself – during a stunning monologue – he raises the prospect of fleeing Rome with Bérénice. That thought, however, so incompatible with Roman glory, would mean his death, as he later says to Bérénice herself.[16]

Bérénice passes through a more complex itinerary of disclosure than Titus does in Racine's drama. She introduces herself to the audience, in interaction with her friend and would-be lover Antiochus, as the empress in waiting. After her period of anxiety, while Titus mourned the death of his father and appeared distant from her, she exults that the new emperor, having deified Vespasian and having already added Syria and Arabia to her realm, will now also crown her success with marriage. When Antiochus confesses his love to her, her personal confidence is so great that she replies she can't believe any mortal could declare his love for her on the very day that she is to be united to Caesar. She softens the blow by resolving not to speak to anyone of Antiochus's impertinence in view of their friendship, but her imperial condescension is palpable. She refuses the warning of her confidante Phénice that Romans accept only Roman women in marriage, and that they detest kings, so the status of being a foreigner and a queen is a scandal. Bérénice replies that Titus can now do as he wishes.[17] In Racine's tragic vision of her, she does not lack hubris.

Titus, however, at this stage knows Bérénice better than she knows herself, remarking to his confidant Paulinus that her heart has only ever asked for his own. She echoes this thought in her encounter with Titus, the same encounter that closes with him leaving the room in a stammer.[18] His evident confusion leads Bérénice to conclude that he has discovered that Antiochus is in love with her, and therefore is jealous. Taking that as a good sign, since it signals Titus's continuing passion, she says that she had counted herself prematurely among those who are unhappy, and sinks deeper into the delusion that her relationship with the new emperor is durable.[19] The decision of Titus to involve Antiochus, of all people, as an intermediary to separate himself from Bérénice only complicates matters further, and complications occupy the bulk of act 3. When Antiochus tells Bérénice that Titus has decided that the couple must part, she responds that she does not believe the report. She dismisses this claim (together with the unfortunate Antiochus) as a trap to split the lovers apart: Titus cannot wish her to die, she insists, which would be the consequence of separation.[20] Only Titus himself can truly explain his decision, which he at last resolves to do.

Titus's last, at first unwelcome, visit to her finds her convinced that he has, in effect, promised to hate her. In her despair, Bérénice tells Titus in person that she had "believed herself loved." She presses him by proposing that, even if he forswears marrying her, she might at least remain near him in Rome. When he calls that an impossible compromise, she prays that in dying she can forget her suffering.[21] Her reaction amounts to a decision to die. Titus's palpable distress, together with a final appearance of Antiochus in the last scene, in the end leads Bérénice to her resolution, and the resolution of the play. She speaks simply and directly, "I thought that your love was about to run its course. I see my error, and you love me always."[22] Her tragic repentance is to acknowledge that she had been loved and was loved, and that for her Rome was beside the point all along.

Racine's writing, precise and moving, features Bérénice's emotional arc as the driving force of the play. The demands on the actress playing the role are considerable, and have been met in our time by performances, both recorded and not, by Carole Bouquet. Her interpretative acumen offers a map for understanding the play in terms of renunciation.[23] To this extent, Racine was guided by

Madeleine de Scudéry's perspective, creating a portrait of relentless – but in the end, tragic – determination without a trace of Juvenal's satire.

Racine's contextualization of Bérénice's central power in Idumea rather than Judea, his routine reference to her as lacking Roman citizenship, when that had been granted her family from the time of Julius Caesar, and his equation of her with Cleopatra are all examples of exoticizing anachronism.[24] He also produces an Antiochus of Commagene more from his imagination than from any identifiable source, and dates Vespasian's death earlier than is plausible in order to make it a psychological motivation for Titus. Yet there is far more invention – together with intrigue and sexual melodrama – in Pierre Corneille's competing play, *Tite et Bérénice,* which presents itself as a "comédie heroïque." Both plays show the influence of Scudéry, but the complications of plot in Corneille's treatment brought stunning criticism, while Racine's work has garnered more performances than Corneille's, much critical praise, and notable operatic adaptations.[25] Racine's focus on Berenice represents progress in making her an active agent of her purposes, even if those purposes are more limited in the play than they were in history.

Yet the undiluted attention to Berenice's passion, compounded with the baroque enhancement of intrigue that Corneille championed, has also fed the view of Berenice as a miniaturized Cleopatra – a view that has been revived in recent representations. The result coarsens both Cleopatra and Berenice. A novelistic portrayal that appeared in 2009 features a naked woman's body preserved in Rome, with her beautiful skin intact and an approximation of Berenice's name tattooed around her navel.[26] Following the approach of *The Da Vinci Code* to Mary Magdalene, the novel has not enjoyed the same reach, but pursues the sort of logic that inspired Dan Brown. In 2024, Berenice was written into *Those About to Die,* a series directed by Roland Emmerich and Marco Kreuzpaintner.[27] In their rendering she is more sexually active than in most treatments, but no more so than several of the other characters, in what is even by recent standards a lubricious effort.

Fiction does not need to observe the constraints of history; its broader latitude permits it to make plain the type of imagination that prevails in the period in which it is produced. Just as the influence of Racine produced a romantic Berenice for modernity, the postmodern Berenice has largely been consigned to a sexualized category. With that charged sexuality, recent claims – putatively historical – have involved her in conspiracies that vary from writing the New Testament with Josephus in order to discredit Judaism and invent Christianity, to maneuvering Nerva into suspending the taxation of Jews.[28] Her capacity to do so came from her character: "powerful, political and pulchritudinous," in the words of one researcher.[29] Juvenal might have envied the alliteration, and he certainly would have agreed with the sentiment.

Literature that speculates about what Berenice might have done, were she motivated in ways familiar today, has been robust, and feeds her myth as a larger than human figure, with appetites and strengths beyond the norm. Mythic representations of her have themselves attracted research interest.[30] But the readiness to understand portrayals of Berenice as mythological indicates an awareness that they are not historical. They trade on what Robin Collingwood, discussed in Chapter 2, called the gossip-value of biography. Berenice's alleged incest with Agrippa II, when it becomes the leading indicator of her significance in history, is an example of that sort of quasi-mythological excursion into what Collingwood called "cattishness."

Juvenal and Josephus joined in the accusation of incest, and their intention was indeed catty. Nonetheless, they write what they write, and their statements need to be assessed. Assessment, however, is not merely a matter of deciding whether a statement can be taken at face value. As Collingwood remarked, "Confronted with a ready-made statement about a subject he is studying, the scientific historian never asks himself: 'Is this statement true or false,' in other words, 'Shall I incorporate it in my history of the subject or not?'"[31] A procedure of that kind, if followed, would fuse all manner of claims, with varying degrees of validity, into an unwieldy amalgam. Rather, the truth of an assertion in history does not lie in whether it is true or false, but in the fact that the assertion is made: why do Josephus and Juvenal write of Berenice's incest when they do? In both cases, Berenice's influence is apparent in the reaction against her. Juvenal feared her Judaism, and Josephus feared her capacity to put his loyalty to Rome in doubt. They both intended to diminish Berenice in the minds of their readers or hearers at a time when her removal from Rome years earlier meant that she was no longer a power to be reckoned with. The allegation of incest itself might well have been directed at her by the Cynic critics whom Titus attempted to silence, as discussed in Chapter 6. By the time his father died and he rose to power, however, Titus had adjusted to the criticisms he had earlier resisted, eager to shed his reputation as a Nero in waiting, and Berenice had returned to Caesarea Philippi.

The accusations of incest, then, reveal efforts to relegate Berenice that are themselves redolent of the political interests in play, and, in their desire to reduce her importance, attest to her influence. Her capacity to excite resistance, as well as her accomplishments, define her life. Berenice has a "life" in this sense, as the sum of the intentions (my preferred term for what Collingwood calls "thoughts") that so affected her contemporaries that they responded. Their responses were often and obviously negative, to the point of demeaning her, but she also aroused a degree of admiration that conformed to her purposes. She became a queen without being born one; she helped shape imperial opinion to the point that she helped bring one emperor, Vespasian, to power, even as she won the passionate affection of another, Titus; and her relationship with Titus brought her dynasty and her religion to Rome, where she embodied them both and where her influence was curried and feared even as it provoked scandal.

Berenice's governing intentions unfolded over the course of her life. Although her marriages can be depicted as arrangements that removed agency from her, two of Berenice's nuptials enhanced the power of her dynasty. Marcus Julius Alexander gave her father the financial backing he needed from Egypt, and his brother, Tiberius Julius Alexander, proved to be of incalculable value in forging an alliance between the Herodians and the Flavians when the revolt against Rome broke out. Marriage to Herod of Chalcis made her a queen, and her two sons represented considerable dynastic capital. Even Berenice's third marriage, to Polemon, broadened the network of allies, involving her however briefly in the governance of lands far from her native Judea. Her relationship with Titus did not make her his wife, although Dio Cassius's complaint that she behaved as if that were the case shows how important it was to her, to Titus, and to opinion in Rome. Had she had her way, which according to Suetonius was also Titus's desire, Herodian power would have reached its incontestable apogee with Berenice.

The episode with Polemon, ill-defined as the sources leave it, underscores Berenice's intentional practice of Judaism; she joined other Herodian women in requiring that prospective husbands be circumcised. The requirement may seem stunning, since in many ways her behavior contradicted what is considered traditional Judaism. Even Josephus, we have seen, said that women could not divorce their husbands according to Judaic practice, although Berenice and several Herodian women (and others outside the family) did just that. During the course of her life, she was involved in the erection of statues to herself, in stamping coins with human images on them, and in celebrating Roman victory with gladiatorial games; she also maintained a sexual relationship with an uncircumcised Roman general, much as her sister Drusilla had in her marriage with the uncircumcised procurator Felix. Berenice's allegiances seem contradictory from the point of view of the Rabbinic Judaism that emerged after her death, during the second century. From her own Herodian perspective, however, her pursuit of power and her dedication to her ancestral religion were complementary. Further, when Rome's agent Gessius Florus threatened the integrity of the Temple in Jerusalem, Berenice confronted him while committing herself to the requirements of a Nazirite vow. She visibly made herself a partisan of the Temple in a way that even Josephus, scarcely her supporter, had to recognize.

Drusilla could not require Felix to accept circumcision; neither did Berenice make that requirement of Titus. Josephus, loyal to his Flavian patrons, does not even mention an affair that provoked resistance in Rome from quarters that finally could not be ignored. The principal concern implicit in Berenice's actions was not circumcision in any case, but marriage to Titus. With that marriage extraordinary advantages would have come: the enhancement of her personal power, the vindication of her dynasty, and the possibility that the Temple in Jerusalem could be restored. Queen Berenice would in effect have become Berenice Augusta, the Roman Empire would have acknowledged the standing of Judaism in way it had not before, and those who practiced Judaism would have had a Temple protected by Rome, as was the case prior to 70 CE.

Berenice's departure from Rome and Titus's unexpected death ruined Berenice's ambition in its ultimate phase. The deaths of influential men in her life became a theme; illness was their nemesis, even when not named. She grieved the passing of Marcus Julius Alexander, Agrippa I, Herod of Chalcis, and now Titus. But assessing the failure of her project necessitates understanding the distinctive intents of its author. Berenice intended to extend her dynasty, which was Maccabean as well as Herodian, in biological and political terms; she intervened in Roman politics both to defend the Temple in Jerusalem and to favor her Flavian friends in their quest for power; and finally, she pursued a relationship with Titus that held the prospect of enhancing, in a spectacular way, both Herodian power and Judaism's standing within the Roman Empire.

Considering Berenice's intents as latent and legible in her actions reveals a person operating for purposes outside the usual run of contemporary experience. She illustrates Collingwood's definition that "historical knowledge is the re-enactment of a past thought encapsulated in a context of present thoughts which, by contradicting it, confines it to a plane different from theirs."[32] Seen in these terms, Berenice indeed operated on a different plane. The contexts of her actions – Second Temple Judaism, Rome's empire, and the Herodian scramble for power – were unlike contemporary contexts in many ways. But she also engaged with those settings as part of her own distinctive agenda – one based on the interests of her dynasty, the Temple's inviolability, and alliance with Roman power. Her combination of political, religious, and personal vectors of power and her commitment to their combination in her hands are unfamiliar in today's world.

Berenice's ambitious goals could not be pursued after Titus's death, and the results of that disappointment were consequential. Herodian power never recovered its former definition and extent;

the issue of the Temple festered; and Rome's relationship with monotheism became both increasingly contentious and worked out more in relation to Christianity than to Judaism.

Agrippa II and Berenice probably lived out their lives in Caesarea Philippi. When Agrippa died, his realm did not pass on to surviving Herodians, but was incorporated under the authority of the legate to Judea, a position that Vespasian and Titus had established. Herodian power no longer directed affairs in the territories of Herod the Great. Some Herodians did maintain influential positions, but elsewhere. Tacitus indicates that Aristobulus, the first son of Herod of Chalcis, was able to gain further territory, as part of the defense of Armenia, under Nero.[33] Also in Armenia, descendants of Herod the Great's son Alexander, whose mother was Mariamme, continued a dynastic line, but without anything like control of the Temple.[34] Clearly, after the war the dynasty did better outside of Judea than within it, and in any case Josephus describes the dynasty as having run its providential course.[35]

In particular, Berenice's sons Berenicianus and Hyrcanus did not benefit from preferential treatment within imperial politics, at least as far as we know. Perhaps a locally important woman named Julia Crispina in a second-century archive, identified as the daughter of a man named Berenicianus, constitutes a reference to one of Berenice's sons and his daughter, but that is a matter of conjecture.[36] In any case, whether or not her sons survived long into adulthood, they did not enjoy the illustrious careers of some of their contemporary relatives. Even when Berenice enjoyed Flavian favor, her children were embarrassments in terms of any imperial succession, since they could be considered competitors for power; when she fell out of favor, they fell further.

Berenice's sons paid the price for her audacity, but audacity ran in the family. Antipater, her great-great-grandfather, committed himself to Rome at a time when others allied with the Parthians. Herod the Great pursued that strategy, and won a royal diadem for his audacious plan to retake Jerusalem after the Parthians had expelled him. Herod's sons, Archelaus and Antipas, had different approaches to regain their father's power, the former by force and the latter by stolid advancement in Roman favor. Berenice's father, Agrippa I, had by the brilliant management of imperial politics regained the throne of his grandfather, and Berenice's own daring plan, had it succeeded, would have been recognized as even more remarkable. When it failed, as has become plain, the attitudes of the new order of Domitian and his successors made Berenice an object of ridicule. Herodian intemperance, a family trait although not a universal one, had brought the dynasty unanticipated success and stunning collapses. The arc of Berenice's life suggests that she shared the disregard for danger that her ancestors displayed, and she paid for pressing her advantages, real and imagined, too far.

The Herodians who continued to rule followed a path quite different from Berenice's. Before her, in Caesarea Philippi, Herod's son Philip outlasted his half-brother Archelaus and avoided the humiliation his half-brother Antipas suffered by means of a diffident attitude of governance: flattering the emperor, making himself useful, and exercising patronage without extending his territory. Agrippa II inherited Philip's lands and shared his governing temperament, which served him well. Precisely what makes him seem less admirable than his sister also helped him to cling to imperial favor in the midst of volatile change. He had no children, and apparently could not advance the children of Berenice. The Herodians who continued their rule into the second century indeed carried on the lineage of Herod the Great and Mariamme, but through their son Alexander, and therefore not through Agrippa I. In any case, their ancestry did not translate into power on the ground in Judea and its associated lands.

The issue of the Temple, left unresolved at the time of Titus's death, returned with violence in the next century. Josephus had articulated his yearning for restoration in 75 in his *Jewish War,* carefully stating where the materials taken from the Sanctuary had been deposited in Rome, at the Temple of Peace and the imperial palace, as if mapping their eventual return. Berenice's marriage to Titus, had it taken place, could have signaled the possibility of realizing such hopes. Policies under Domitian and subsequent emperors, however, who supported traditional Roman religion, meant that imperial support for the project could not be expected. Totally apart from Rome a Jewish leader named Simon bar Kosibah took the name Bar Kokhba (son of a star) to indicate that he fulfilled the prophecy of Israel's vindication in Numbers 24:17. He organized the revolt of 132–135, which was centered on the Temple and its renewed operation. The Roman response was even more comprehensively destructive than the reaction in 70. Still, when Julian became emperor, he was eager to encourage traditional sacrificial practices and to resist Christianity, and authorized the rebuilding of the Temple – but his death in battle with the Sassanids in 363 prevented completion of the project.[37] The unsettled matter of the of the Temple opened possibilities for building it again until annexation later by Muslim, Crusader, and again Muslim rulers; efforts to rededicate the site again today for sacrificial worship according to the Torah indicate that the matter is still unresolved as well as provocative.[38]

Julian was determined to reverse the course of Constantine before him in regard to Christianity. When he wrote *Against the Galileans,* one of his objections was the claim that Jesus ontologically was God. His uncle Constantine had sponsored this view in the

Nicene Creed, and Julian was personally acquainted with Gregory Nazianzus, an architect of Trinitarian thought. On Julian's analysis, any claim that identified "the Most High God" with one person was nonsense, a form of monotheism so limited that it no longer represented God. Rather, in his Neoplatonic conception, the true God above all things and thoughts could be perceived as reflected in the various religions that Rome had inherited.

Judaism was one of those religions, and Julian believed that, although misguided, it was preferable to Christianity. To assert that the God of Israel was the only god was a contradiction in Neoplatonic terms, because there are gods and angels of many peoples. Yet Julian was interested in tolerating traditional beliefs under the umbrella of the ethnic diversity of the Roman Empire and his personal conviction that the divine truth beyond all individual deities shined through them. Christianity, neither an ancient practice nor the custom of a definable ethnic constituency of his realm, could no longer be preferred in his view.

Julian's public support for the rebuilding of the Temple in Jerusalem is portrayed in some Christian accounts as a spiteful gesture against Christianity. But at the time he took up his position of support, Judaism was about as well represented demographically as Christianity was, and its legal standing was centuries old. Julian was well aware, as well, of the centrality of the Temple in the revolts against Rome in 66 CE and 132 CE. His letter to the Jewish community as a whole expresses his concern for their welfare, and suspends taxes that had been levied since the time of the revolts.[39] The logic had been that the annual payment by Jews for the upkeep of the Temple should be co-opted by Rome. Reversing that arrangement opened up adequate resources to bring the new project to completion, had Julian lived.

Julian's policy involved not merely recognizing the practice of Judaism; he proceeded to approve and encourage its practice within the bounds of his particular kind of Neoplatonism. A learned politician and general, he also probably knew the story of Titus and Berenice. Whether or not he thought of their relationship as a precedent that favored the rebuilding of the Temple in Jerusalem, Julian did explicitly conceive of Judaism as a viable religion within his policy of general tolerance. That is, he wished to incorporate a monotheist religion within the panoply of traditions that reached back in his view to the Most High God. Philip Freeman has argued that, had he lived, Julian would have prevented Christianity from becoming the religion of Rome.[40] That was clearly part of his intent, but he also presented the prospect of a closer incorporation of Judaism within a philosophically revised Roman pantheon.

Berenice benefited from nothing like Julian's education, and is rendered inarticulate by the historical sources that mention her. As a result, her views of the Judaism that she fiercely defended are unknown. Her defense of the Temple, however, shows that within all her commitments, her natural and instinctive loyalties never wavered in support of the project her great-grandfather had made possible. Attempts in recent years to give her relationships with prominent figures in later, Rabbinic Judaism have been pursued only in fiction, and all the evidence suggests they must remain in that idiom. But just as Berenice was ambitious for herself and her dynasty to an extent that ultimately undermined her reputation in Rome, so her dedication to the Temple stands in implicit tension with her routinely philo-Roman behavior. Had she succeeded in her project of marrying Titus, Rome might well have accommodated to a form of monotheism quite unlike the Trinitarian theology that came later, and from a new religion. She did not theorize, as far as the sources indicate, about what such an accommodation would have meant, and it is impossible to know whether or how she would have taken the opportunity to theorize at all.

In his own sphere, Titus operated with magnificent energy, pursuing his father's initiatives in the case of dedicating the Colosseum in 80 CE. The project had proceeded with wealth taken from the Temple in Jerusalem, so the dedication might have marked a moment for defining a fresh purpose. But war in Britain and the eruption of Vesuvius, together with fire and plague in Rome, occupied Titus fully until his death. Like Berenice, his life was crafted from his bold reaction to events rather than from his own carefully laid plans or from well-developed theories of governance.

After Titus died, Berenice's trail goes cold, except for gossipy remarks that are retrospective and crafted in relation to the men around her. The strange partnership of Josephus and Juvenal insists on her incestuous sexuality, while Suetonius and Dio Cassius characterize her dismissively. At least Tacitus and Quintilian manage anodyne comments that may amount to grudging respect. If she lived another twenty years after leaving Rome, she reached the age of seventy. Time enough for her to wonder whether she had done all she could for her dynasty, for the Temple, and for the lover who featured so centrally in her ambitions. Titus himself, Suetonius said, sometimes remarked "I have lost a day" if he realized he had not done good for anyone during his waking hours.[41] Suetonius and his colleagues would never have thought of attributing such sentiments to Berenice, yet she evidently had lost no time in pursuing her life's end. Her efforts did not produce definitive change or unqualified success, but in helping to shape the events of a pivotal century, she has left legible traces of a consequential life.

Chronology

BCE

47	Julius Caesar installs Cleopatra as queen of Egypt, Herod the Great's father Antipater as procurator of Judea, the Maccabean Hyrcanus as ethnarch, and Sextus Caesar as governor of Syria
44	Caesar's assassination on the Ides of March
43	Formation of the Second Triumvirate of Antony, Octavian, and Lepidus; the assassination of Antipater
42	Antony and Octavian defeat Brutus and Cassius at Philippi
40	To counter the Parthians and their collaborators in Judea, Antony and Octavian have Herod named king of Judea before the Senate in Rome
37	The effective beginning of Herod's reign, after defeating the Parthian threat, and of his marriage to the Maccabean princess Mariamme I
29	Herod's execution of Mariamme I
27	Octavian becomes "Imperator Caesar Augustus," while Herod marries the Samaritan Malthake (the mother of Archelaus and Antipas) and founds Sebaste in Samaria in honor of Augustus
23	Herod's sons by Mariamme, Alexander and Aristobulus, depart for Rome
17	The return of Alexander and Aristobulus from Rome
12	Augustus's meeting with Herod and his sons Antipater, Alexander, and Aristobulus to resolve the contentious issue of succession
7	Herod's execution of his sons Alexander and Aristobulus
4	On the death of Herod the Great, Augustus divides his realm among his sons Archelaus, Antipas, and Philip

CE

6	The removal of Archelaus from office in the midst of a tax revolt led by Judas the Galilean; accepting the view of the Sadducees, Augus-

	tus appoints a Roman prefect to administer Judea in the midst of a census under Quirinius, the legate to Syria
14	The death of Augustus and the accession of Tiberius
19	Antipas dedicates the new city of Tiberias
ca. 21	The beheading of John the Baptist at Antipas's order
23	The death of Tiberius's son Drusus leaves Herod's grandson Agrippa I bereft of his most important imperial friend
ca. 25	Agrippa I comes to Tiberias as the city's agoranomos
26	Pontius Pilate named prefect of Judea, as Tiberius retires to Capri, leaving Rome to Sejanus, prefect of the Praetorian Guard
27	Antipas's first efforts to have Jesus killed
ca. 28	The birth of Berenice
31	The death of Sejanus in Rome
32	Jesus's arrest and execution in Jerusalem with Antipas's involvement; the conversion of Paul
ca. 33	Departure of Agrippa I and Cyprus from Tiberias
34	The death of Philip, Herod the Great's son
37	The death of Tiberius; the accession of Caligula with the promotion of Agrippa I to become king of Gaulanitis and associated territories; the removal of Pontius Pilate from power; the birth of Josephus
38	Berenice's marriage contract with Marcus Julius Alexander, son of the alabarch of Alexandria
39	Antipas is deposed from power by Caligula, who extends Agrippa I's territory
40	Caligula orders that his statue be erected in the Temple in Jerusalem
41	The assassination of Caligula, and Claudius's accession with the help of Agrippa I; the new emperor names Agrippa I king of Herod the Great's territories, and his brother Herod as king of Chalcis
44	The death of Marcus Julius Alexander; Berenice's marriage to Herod of Chalcis; and the death Agrippa I, with Cuspius Fadus named as procurator of Judea
ca. 45	The insurrection of Theudas; in Antioch, followers of Jesus in Antioch begin to be commonly called "Christians"

Chronology

46–48	The procurator Tiberius Julius Alexander, Berenice's relative by her first marriage, enhances the influence of Herod of Chalcis and Berenice in Jerusalem and deals with the consequences of famine
48	The death of Herod of Chalcis, and the replacement of Tiberius Julius Alexander with Ventidius Cumanus
52	The appointment of Felix as procurator of Judea
53	Agrippa II appointed king in Caesarea Philippi; the marriage of Berenice's sister Drusilla to Azizus, king of Emesa
54	The death of Claudius, the accession of Nero; Drusilla divorces Azizus to marry the Roman procurator Felix
ca. 56	Berenice's marriage to Polemon, king of Pontus, Colchis, and Cilicia
ca. 57	Berenice's return to Caesarea Philippi; Paul announces his decision to visit Jerusalem in his Letter to the Romans
59	Festus replaces Felix, sending Paul on to Rome in consultation with Agrippa II and Berenice
62	The death by stoning of the Nazirite James, the brother of Jesus, in Jerusalem as Albinus makes his way to Jerusalem after the death of Festus
ca. 63	The Areopagus inscription, designed to identity a statue of Queen Berenice
64	The appointment of Gessius Florus as procurator; the fire in Rome, followed by Nero's pogrom against Christians
66	After Berenice's Nazirite vow and appeal for peace, the priestly administrator in the Temple refuses to accept the emperor's offerings; Cestius Gallus, the Roman legate in Syria, retreats after attempting to secure Jerusalem with Agrippa II
67	The relationship between Titus and Berenice begins in Caesarea Philippi
68	The death of Nero
69	The accession of Vespasian, after Galba, Otho, and Vitellius
70	The destruction of Jerusalem and the Temple under Titus
71	The triumph of Vespasian and Titus celebrated in Rome
73	The fall of Masada
75	Dedication of the Temple of Peace in Rome; Agrippa II and Berenice

	are received in Rome under Flavian protection; dissemination of Josephus's *Jewish War*
79	Vespasian's death, and the accession of Titus, with Berenice's departure from Rome
81	The death of Titus; his brother Domitian comes to power and dedicates the Arch of Titus
93–94	Josephus distributes his *Jewish Antiquities*
96	The assassination of Domitian
ca. 100	The dissemination of Josephus's *Life;* the deaths of Agrippa II and Berenice

Genealogy

BERENICE'S HERODIAN LINEAGE,
WITH SOME IMPORTANT RELATIONS
Antipater (Procurator)
with Cyprus
KING HEROD ("THE GREAT")
with Mariamme
with Malthake
with Cleopatra of Jerusalem
Alexander
Aristobulus
with Berenice
Archelaus (Ethnarch)
Antipas (Tetrarch)
Philip (Tetrarch)
Herodias (married Antipas)
KING AGRIPPA I
with Cyprus
King Agrippa II
Drusus
Mariamme
Drusilla
with King Herod of Chalcis, QUEEN BERENICE
with Marcus Julius Alexander, King Polemon, and Titus: no children
Berenicianus
Hyrcanus

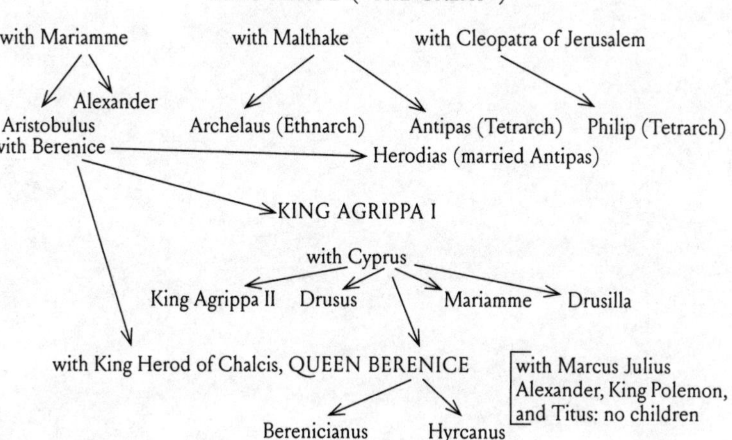

Source Notes

The Source Notes refer to the primary evidence for the discussion. The Bibliography gives preferred editions, usually chosen because they provide original texts as well as translations, although renderings in this book are my own.

INTRODUCTION

Josephus is unquestionably the most important and complete source for understanding his contemporary Berenice, biased though he undoubtedly is. His *Jewish War* entered circulation in 75 CE; his *Jewish Antiquities* during the winter of 93–94. Rich discussion as well as a translation are available in the collection edited by Steve Mason. Both those works of Josephus are in Greek, although Josephus claims in *Jewish War* 1 § 3 that he previously circulated a version of that work in Aramaic. Juvenal's sixth satire is a classic of Latin prose, written around 117 CE, while Quintilian's *Orator's Education* comes from two decades earlier, near the time of Josephus's *Antiquities*. Dio Cassius's *Roman History* was written early in the third century. As the Notes and Bibliography reflect, Grace Harriet Macurdy and Tal Ilan have been key modern contributors to the discussion of Berenice.

CHAPTER 1. CHILD BRIDE IN ALEXANDRIA

Alexandria and the events there that proved pivotal for the Herodians, and Jews of that and other cities, are analyzed in Sandra Gambetti, *The Alexandrian Riots of 38 C.E. and the Persecution of the Jews*. The influence of the Septuagint is traced in an interesting way by Abraham Wasserstein and David Wasserstein in their *Legend of the Septuagint*. The formative period of the Herodians, which preceded Berenice's birth, is described in Josephus's *Jewish Antiquities*, books 14–17, and the initial section of book 18. I have offered only a précis of a rich, complicated, and riveting history, which has been the focus of considerable investigation in recent years, chiefly by means of a critical examination of Josephus's works. In the Bibliography, see in particular the contributions of Daniel R. Schwartz, Nikos Kokkinos, Julia Wilker, Bruce Chilton, and Martin Goodman. Of course those works provide details of wider literature. Once the period of Berenice's immediate family is reached, Philo of Alexandria's *Embassy to Gaius* becomes a very welcome supplement to Josephus's account.

Source Notes

CHAPTER 2. QUEEN OF CHALCIS

Because Josephus was born in 37 CE, events toward the end of the period described in this chapter were easily within living memory of people he knew. Philo's contributions, by contrast, do not continue after 40 CE, which is often surmised as commencing the decade of his death. Despite a very terse style and a date during the early second century (106–107 CE in the case of the *Histories*, 115 in the case of the *Annals*), Tacitus provides corresponding evidence, as does Dio Cassius from the third century. Discussion is available in Woodman, *Cambridge Companion to Tacitus;* and Lange and Madsen, *Cassius Dio*. Tacitus and Dio Cassius prove increasingly important as Berenice comes into focus as an individual later in her life. The New Testament's book of Acts is an eclectic source that has been variously dated between 90 and 120. A dating within that period would make sense of its intellectual interest in framing an account designed for the tastes of a movement known the Second Sophistic, which aimed at incorporating Greek inheritances of rhetoric and culture within the hegemonic claims of the Roman Empire. In this regard, see Nasrallah, "Acts of the Apostles," 533–566. Daniel R. Schwartz devoted a monograph to Agrippa I, offering a good foundation for analysis. See Schwartz, *Agrippa I*.

CHAPTER 3. SISTER OF AGRIPPA II

Photius is available in a critical edition by René Henry, cited in the Bibliography; see Photius, *Bibliothèque*. Tacitus in this case is a notable witness, since he shows awareness of the difficulties under Cumanus long after the fact. He no doubt regards events from the perspective of the time after the war that broke out in 66 CE, but it is notable that he sees the two periods in comparable terms. The splendor of Caesarea Philippi is depicted in both academic and popular works. See Friedland, *Roman Marble Sculptures;* Wilson, *Caesarea Philippi*.

CHAPTER 4. WIFE OF KING POLEMON

Suetonius remains an indispensable source, although his proclivity to shape the materials available to him is well acknowledged. See Wardle, "Suetonius," 101–115; Power and Gibson, *Suetonius the Biographer*. Because Paul allegedly comes to voice in his own right in Acts, the presentation of Paul there has been a topic of lively discussion, and the conclusion follows that Acts also shapes its sources; see Schellenberg, "First Pauline Chronologist?" 193–213. In the case of Josephus, the recourse to sources has been well documented (although the identity of the sources is not a matter of complete agreement), along with the additional feature that, as brilliantly shown by Daniel R. Schwartz in his article "*Kata Touton ton Kairon*," the conflation of sources results in conflations of time.

Source Notes

CHAPTER 5. PENITENT IN JERUSALEM

Although Suetonius is a programmatic writer, his program is not the same as that of Josephus, so that one might be used to correct and/or reinforce the other. See Wardle, "Suetonius," 101–115; Power and Gibson, *Suetonius the Biographer*. Eusebius, a fourth-century historian of Christianity, was inspired by an agenda to depict the providential triumph that in his mind Constantine represented. He also had recourse to earlier sources, notably Hegesippus from the second century, whom he references in relation to James, the brother of Jesus. These are detailed in the edition cited. The study of Josephus's perspective, both internally in reference to his own corpus of writing, and externally in relation to other ancient sources, has been intensively studied over the past fifty years in particular. See Chapman and Rodgers, *Companion to Josephus*.

CHAPTER 6. TITUS'S PARAMOUR IN ROME

The "Jewish War," named after the title of Josephus's account, has been detailed in *History of the Jewish War,* the comprehensive treatment by Steve Mason. Owing to Josephus's studied silence in regard to Berenice in her relationship, recourse to Suetonius, Tacitus, Dio Cassius, Plutarch, and related works becomes indispensable. Fortunately, Josephus does provide indications of chronology that permit a coordination among the various sources, each of which requires assessment according to its agenda, discussed here as necessary.

EPILOGUE

Racine's *Bérénice* is available in many editions in a host of languages and adaptations. I have used the enumerated lines of Paul Fièvre in *Théâtre Classique.* It is based on Racine, *Bérénice,* the edition by Claude Barbin in which Racine's own remarks help to contextualize the work. Notes provide further reference to related works, secondary literature, and to the remarkable performance of Carole Bouquet in the role of Bérénice. The contentious history of the site of the Second Temple is analyzed in Fine, *Temple of Jerusalem.*

Notes

INTRODUCTION

1. See Juvenal, *Satires* 6.155–158, incisively discussed in Watson, "Flight of Pudicitia," 62–79.

2. Elegantly described in Macurdy, "Julia Berenice," 246–253, and Freisenbruch, "Little Cleopatra," 133–154. Mommsen's famous comment appears in his *Römische Geschichte,* 5:539.

3. Quintilian's claim, assessed further in Chapter 6, appears in *Orator's Education* 4.1.19, and Dio Cassius's remark in his *Roman History* 65.15.3–5.

4. Juvenal, *Satires* 14.96–99.

5. Macurdy, *Vassal-Queens,* 84n99, dates the inscription to 61 CE, but Theogenos's predecessor, Tiberius Claudius Novius, appears to have died in that year or the next. Tiberius Claudius Theogenos of Paiania came later; see Geagan, "Tiberius Claudius Novius," 279–287, esp. 286–287. See too the dating of Schmalz, *Augustan and Julio-Claudian Athens,* 128, and the discussion in Ilan, *Queen Berenice,* 69–71. For attempts to portray Berenice's title as derivative, see Macurdy, "Julia Berenice," 248, and Ilan, *Queen Berenice,* 66. First published by Jacob Spon, the dedication appears in the mammoth and long-standing project *Inscriptiones Graecae;* see *Inscriptiones Graecae II et III,* entry 3449 (superseding earlier enumerations). I am most grateful to Sebastian Prignitz, head of the project, for his attempts to trace the now lost inscription.

CHAPTER 1. CHILD BRIDE IN ALEXANDRIA

1. Philo, *Embassy to Gaius* § 338, in *Philo;* Suetonius, Gaius Caligula 49.2–3, in Suetonius, *Lives of the Caesars.*

2. See Philo, *Life of Moses* 2.15–16 §§ 73–76, in *Philo;* and Martens, *One God, One Law.*

3. Philo, *Special Laws* 1.1–2, in *Philo.*

4. Josephus, *Jewish Antiquities* 14 §§ 403–404.

5. See Goodman, *Herod the Great,* 67–68. Herod's dynastic stratagem in marrying Mariamme is a conclusion endorsed by Goodman on 45–46, agreeing with Chilton, *The Herods,* 86–88. As I pointed out there, 37 BCE was a conjugal year, since Antony

and Cleopatra also stepped further into public awareness that year as a couple; see Ager, "Marriage or Mirage?," 139–155. Cleopatra's reported later attempt to seduce Herod in the interests of winkling from him prime lands around the Jordan River contributed to her vampish reputation; see Chilton, *The Herods,* 89–99; Goodman, *Herod the Great,* 51.

6. Josephus, *Jewish Antiquities* 15 §§ 202–239.

7. The execution of Herod's sons is reported in Josephus, *Jewish Antiquities* 16 §§ 356–394. Augustus's remark is attested only much later, by Marcobius in his fifth-century *Saturnalia* 2.4.11, but Jordan D. Rosenblum has shown how well it fits the period to which it is attributed; See Rosenblum, "'Why Do You Refuse to Eat Pork?'" 95–110.

8. Leviticus 18:16 made Antipas's marriage to Herodias unacceptable; her plot against John the Baptist appears in Mark 6:14–29 and Matthew 14:1–12. Josephus's account in *Jewish Antiquities* 18 §§ 116–119 is more sober, although it is he who gives a name to Salome in § 136. There is a rich discussion of the history, art, and literature involving Salome; see the helpful, visually striking introduction available in Kultermann, "'Dance of the Seven Veils,'" 187–215.

9. Agrippa's appointment in Tiberias is related in Josephus, *Jewish Antiquities* 18 §§ 147–150, a source that also explains the controversy in regard to the city's alleged uncleanness in §§ 36–38.

10. Agrippa's accusation for bribery is recounted in Josephus, *Jewish Antiquities* 18 §§ 150–158, while the death of Flaccus appears in Tacitus, *Annals,* 6.27; see *Tacitus.*

11. Josephus, *Jewish Antiquities* 18 §§ 159–165. Antonia's remarkable influence is detailed in Kokkinos, *Antonia Augusta.*

12. Josephus, *Jewish Antiquities* 18 § 160.

13. Josephus, *Jewish Antiquities* 18 §§ 166–204.

14. Josephus, *Jewish War* 2 § 181; *Jewish Antiquities* 18 § 237.

15. Josephus, *Jewish Antiquities* 18 §§ 238–239.

16. Philo, *Flaccus* §§ 25–35, in *Philo.*

17. Philo, *Flaccus* §§ 36–40, in *Philo.*

18. Ilan, *Queen Berenice,* 65. Ilan makes it clear (on 62–64, for example) that she is contesting Ruth Jordan's *Berenice,* which portrays an eagerly "philadelphic" Berenice. I agree with Ilan's program, but also think that at times it is anachronistic. When, for instance, she says of Cyprus as a model for Berenice that while Agrippa I "traveled; she stayed home tending the children" (64) and that later Berenice occupied herself "having babies and raising them" (65), that may have been the case, but only episodically. Ilan (193) has Berenice "married" to Marcus Julius Alexander only from 42, al-

though she places the betrothal in 38 (52). She also exacerbates the issue of the discrepancy in age in the couple, saying that Marcus Julius Alexander might have been married a time or two prior to his marriage to Berenice (53).

19. See Meshorer, *Treasury of Jewish Coins,* 231. Ilan's monograph *Queen Berenice* offers a fine survey of archeological, numismatic, and genealogical evidence, all with appropriate bibliography. Her compendium of "Berenice's Foremothers" (21–45) is a wonderful resource, although it needs to be kept in mind that during the period of Second Temple Judaism, Judaic ancestry was reckoned as a rule in patrilineal rather than matrilineal terms. See Regev, "Herod's Jewish Ideology," 197–222. Conditions after the arson of the Temple in 70 CE and its comprehensive destruction in 135 are reflected in the changed approach to lineage in Rabbinic Judaism. Josephus's interest in identifying the line of descent through the daughters of Herod (*Jewish Antiquities* 18 §§ 130–141) is striking in this regard.

20. Josephus, *Jewish Antiquities* 15 §§ 259–266.

CHAPTER 2. QUEEN OF CHALCIS

1. Josephus, *Jewish Antiquities* 18 §§ 240–255.

2. Philo, *Embassy to Gaius* §§ 200–202, in *Philo.*

3. Josephus, *Jewish Antiquities* 19 § 276.

4. See Tacitus, *Histories* 5.9, in *Tacitus*—corresponding to the reaction described in Philo, *Embassy to Gaius* §§ 203–208—as well as Josephus, *Jewish War* 2 §§ 184–203, and Josephus, *Jewish Antiquities* 18 §§ 257–288.

5. Josephus, *Jewish Antiquities* 18 §§ 289–301.

6. Philo, *Embassy to Gaius* § 293, cf. Plato, *Timaeus* 28c, in *Plato in Twelve Volumes;* the scene is set in *Embassy to Gaius* §§ 261–333.

7. Josephus, *Jewish Antiquities* 18 §§ 302–304.

8. Philo, *Embassy to Gaius* §§ 337–348; cf. Tacitus, *Histories* 5.9, and Tacitus, *Annals* 12.54, in *Tacitus.*

9. Suetonius, Gaius Caligula 49.2–3, in Suetonius, *Lives of the Caesars;* Philo, *Embassy to Gaius* § 338.

10. Philo, *Embassy to Gaius* §§ 334–335.

11. Suetonius, Gaius Caligula 56–58, in Suetonius, *Lives of the Caesars;* cf. Josephus, *Jewish Antiquities* 19 §§ 1–126.

12. Josephus, *Jewish Antiquities* 19 § 299.

13. The situation is nicely summarized in Goodman, *Herod the Great,* 159–163.

Owing to Goodman's focus on Herod in particular, he does not consider Archelaus as the likely agent of the massacre, an alternative that is set out in Chilton, *The Herods,* 119–140. An anonymous reviewer for *Publishers Weekly* (August 2021), aghast that anyone but the commonly known Herod the Great should be guilty of the Slaughter of the Innocents, assumes that any other argument is not historically accurate, but offers no evidence for that conclusion.

14. Josephus, *Jewish Antiquities* 19 § 357.

15. Reflected in the remarkable "Letter of Claudius to the Alexandrians," published in *Select Papyri,* 2:78–89.

16. See Dio Cassius, *Roman History* 60.6.6, in regard to the restrictions, and Suetonius, Claudius 25.4 (in Suetonius, *Lives of the Caesars*), for the effects on followers of Jesus's movement.

17. See Kropp, "Crowning the Emperor," 377–389; Reinach and Hill, *Jewish Coins,* 36; Madden, *Coins of the Jews,* 136–137. Kropp associates the coin with *Antiquities* 19 § 274. In my opinion the coin is a stylized representation of the speeches that Agrippa and Herod gave before the Senate; Dio Cassius, *Roman History* 60.8.2–3. One reason Agrippa used only his own name was that his brother Herod had also been named a king, and naturally used that designation. Still, Agrippa was quite clear that he was the "great" king, which helps explain why Josephus calls him "Agrippa the Great." He was not content with being the equal of his grandfather; he wanted to supersede him.

18. Josephus, *Jewish Antiquities* 18 § 237; 19 §§ 294–296.

19. The founding is mentioned in Josephus, *Jewish War* 1 §§ 87, 416, and the inscription on the gate of the Temple in Josephus, *Jewish War* 1 § 416.

20. See Roddaz, *Marcus Agrippa,* 456–463; Kokkinos, *Herodian Dynasty,* 271–272; Goodman, *Herod the Great,* 63–66. The hecatomb is mentioned in Josephus, *Antiquities* 16 §§ 13–15.

21. Dio Cassius, *Roman History* 65.4.

22. Suetonius, Julius Caesar 84.5, in Suetonius, *Lives of the Caesars.*

23. An influential biographer of Herod the Great, Abraham Schalit, argued for the king's motivation in terms of the realpolitik of Jews living under Roman rule; see Schalit, *König Herodes.* His work is both a landmark study and a matter of some contention, with interesting implications for historiography. These are discussed in Schwartz, "On Abraham Schalit," 9–28. Schwartz also contributed the foreword to the 2001 edition of Schalit's book. Schalit's own changes of position are in some ways comparable to those of Josephus, but they also indicate how complex the relationship between Judaism and Roman rule could be. I take the view that particular cases need to be assessed without any assumption that Judaism either opposed Rome or endorsed its hegemony. Evidence for both those attitudes, and a host of nuances in between, is too

plentiful to make any default position plausible. In regard to the influence of his background in Tarsus upon Paul, see Chilton, *Rabbi Paul,* 22–27, 233–236.

24. I follow Schwartz, *Agrippa I,* 11–17, in discerning a conflation on Josephus's part at this point, as occurs elsewhere in his corpus. In regard to the Nazirite vow, see Chepey, *Nazirites in Late Second Temple Judaism.* Agrippa's involvement in the vow is reflected in Josephus, *Jewish Antiquities* 19 § 294.

25. Josephus, *Jewish Antiquities* 19 §§ 332–334.

26. Josephus, *Jewish Antiquities* 19 §§ 354, 357.

27. For the theory that Berenice was Agrippa II's lover, see Jordan, *Berenice,* 101–103. For the theory that he was homosexual and had an aversion to physical contact with females, see Ilan, *Queen Berenice,* 73–75.

28. Collingwood, *Principles of History,* 67, 70–71, and *Principles of Art,* 87. Caution in accepting his criticisms is notably urged by his own editors; see *Principles of History,* xxxviii–xli, and Johnson, "R. G. Collingwood on Biography," 125–167.

29. Cf. Fuks, "Marcus Julius Alexander," 10–17, as well as the discussion in Tcherikover and Fuks, *Corpus Papyorum Judaicorum,* 2:197–200. The ostraca are dated between 37 and 43/44 CE and reflect the continuing commercial activity of the alabarch's son, which Fuks assesses together with Josephus's account. Building on his work, Katherine Evans has provided a chronology of the alabarch, in which he was born circa 15–10 BCE, which means that assuming his son Marcus Julius Alexander died of anything like old age in 44 CE seems most precarious; see Evans, "Alexander the Alabarch," 576–594.

30. Josephus, *Jewish Antiquities* 19 § 277.

CHAPTER 3: SISTER OF AGRIPPA II

1. Josephus, *Jewish Antiquities* 19 §§ 297–311.

2. Josephus, *Jewish Antiquities* 19 §§ 326–327.

3. Josephus, *Jewish Antiquities* 19 §§ 335–345.

4. Josephus, *Jewish Antiquities* 19 §§ 346–352.

5. See Acts 12:23. Herod the Great's symptoms are set out in Josephus, *Jewish Antiquities* 17 §§ 146–148, 168–172, in a way that also articulates Josephus's moral judgment; see Ladouceur, "Death of Herod the Great," 25–34. For a clinical discussion, see Hirschman et al., "Death of an Arabian Jew," 833–841. In *The Herods,* 114, 302n79, I suggested Founier's Gangrene as the cause of death, and made the link with Agrippa I's condition. The quick onset of symptoms is a key factor; see Leslie, Rad, and Foreman, "Fournier Gangrene." Genetics-related explanations do not appear to be as likely as co-

morbidity, given the evidence in the literature. Neither Herod the Great nor Agrippa I was innocent of practices that might have contributed to circulatory failure or diabetes, for example.

6. Josephus, *Jewish Antiquities* 19 §§ 354–359.

7. See Photius, *Bibliothèque*, 238, and Ilan, *Queen Berenice*, 60–62. In the end Ilan overcomes the temptation, however, by pointing out that there is no reason to think that Berenice was in Caesarea Maritima at that time. But that reasoning also applies to her sisters, so the suggestion as a whole should probably be seen as a fault in Photius's reading of Josephus. The conditions in which the *Bibliotheka* were composed make that a real possibility; see Treadgold, *Nature of the Bibliotheca of Photius*.

8. Josephus, *Jewish Antiquities* 20 §§ 1–5.

9. Josephus, *Jewish War* 2 §§ 218–220; Josephus, *Jewish Antiquities* 19 §§ 360–363.

10. See Acts 5:36 and Josephus, *Jewish Antiquities* 20 §§ 97–98.

11. Josephus, *Jewish Antiquities* 20 §§ 1–16.

12. The incident of the shields is related in Philo, *Embassy to Gaius* §§ 299–308, in *Philo;* Josephus, *Jewish War* 2 §§ 169–174; and Josephus, *Jewish Antiquities* 18 §§ 55–59; while the events connected with Pilate's confiscation of Temple funds are reflected in Josephus, *Jewish War* 2 §§ 175–177; Josephus, *Jewish Antiquities* 18 §§ 60–62; and Luke 13:1.

13. Josephus, *Jewish Antiquities* 18 §§ 85–89.

14. Josephus, *Jewish Antiquities* 20 §§ 15–16.

15. See Appelbaum, "On the Apostasy," 47–76. Well researched and carefully considered, this article successfully shows how modern preconceptions about Judaism as a religion of the powerless have contributed to the assumption that those practitioners who advanced in power and status were less Jewish than others.

16. Josephus, *Jewish War* 2 § 220.

17. Josephus, *Jewish Antiquities* 20 §§ 100–103.

18. Josephus, *Jewish Antiquities* 20 § 13.

19. Josephus, *Jewish Antiquities* 19 § 353.

20. Josephus, *Jewish Antiquities* 18 §§ 134.

21. Josephus, *Jewish Antiquities* 20 §§ 103–104.

22. Josephus, *Jewish Antiquities* 20 §§ 105–133.

23. Tacitus, *Annals* 12.54, in *Tacitus*.

24. Josephus, *Jewish Antiquities* 20 §§ 135–137.

25. See such suggestions in Kokkinos, *Herodian Dynasty,* 319–320; Jacobson, *Agrippa II,* 173–177; and Ilan, *Queen Berenice,* 64.

26. Josephus, *Jewish Antiquities* 20 § 138.

27. Josephus, *Jewish War* 3 §§ 513–515. For context, see Wilson, *Caesarea Philippi,* 16–17. Philip's coins also indicate his greater accommodation to Hellenistic practice. Unlike Antipas, he even combined his own image with that of Augustus on occasion; see Kindler, "Coin of Herod Philip," 161–163.

28. Josephus, *Jewish Antiquities* 18 §§ 106–108.

CHAPTER 4. WIFE OF KING POLEMON

1. See Tacitus, *Annals* 12.66–69, in *Tacitus;* Dio Cassius, *Roman History* 61.34–35; Suetonius, Claudius 44, in Suetonius, *Lives of the Caesars;* Josephus, *Jewish Antiquities* 20 § 148.

2. Josephus, *Jewish War* 2 §§ 114–116.

3. Josephus, *Jewish Antiquities* 20 §§ 138–144.

4. Josephus, *Jewish Antiquities* 20 §§ 141–143, cf. Tacitus, *Histories* 5.9, in *Tacitus;* Tacitus, *Annals* 12.54.

5. See Jacobson, "Coins," 73–96, esp. 86–87.

6. Josephus, *Jewish Antiquities* 15 §§ 259–266, and see §§ 81–87 for her treatment of a previous husband, Joseph.

7. Brewer, "Jewish Women Divorcing," 349–357; Brooten, "Könnten Frauen im alten Judentum die Scheidung betreiben?," 65–80.

8. Josephus, *Jewish Antiquities* 16 §§ 220–226.

9. Christine Hayes, following John Endres, points out that the suggestion that circumcision might facilitate intermarriage is not dealt with in the book of Jubilees, which rejects intermarriage generally; see Hayes, "Intermarriage and Impurity," 21–25, and Endres, *Biblical Interpretation,* 129.

10. Josephus, *Jewish Antiquities* 15 §§ 267–291.

11. Josephus, *Jewish Antiquities* 19 § 355; 20 §§ 140, 147.

12. His description of the schools appears in Josephus, *Jewish Antiquities* 18 §§ 11–25, and his claim to know them all is in Josephus, *Life* §§ 7–12, in *Flavius Josephus.*

13. See Blanton, "Expressive Prepuce," 127–161.

14. See Berthelot, "*Rabbis Write Back!*," 165–192.

15. Josephus, *Jewish Antiquities* 20 § 145.

16. See Barrett, "Polemo II," 437–448, 444n42. Wilker, *Für Rom und Jerusalem,* 32–33, puts the marriage in 63 CE, and Ilan, *Queen Berenice,* 87, in 64. Kokkinos, *Herodian Dynasty,* 381–382, also puts it in the 60s. The argument in regard to Polemon's demotion appears in Schürer, *History of the Jewish People,* 450n34. Although this position is often repeated, it is fallacious; the demotion itself is dated between 62 and 65.

17. As Josephus puts it in *Jewish Antiquities* 20 § 146, *di' akolosian.*

18. Josephus, *Jewish Antiquities* 20 §§ 145–146.

19. Josephus, *Jewish Antiquities* 20 § 143.

20. Schwartz, *Agrippa I,* 258, and Ilan, *Queen Berenice,* 78.

21. Josephus, *Jewish Antiquities* 20 § 146.

22. The coins of Polemon indicate that he publicly celebrated Julia Mamaea as his "queen" by the 60s CE. Obviously, Berenice had departed by that time. See Barrett, "Polemo II," 437–448, and Sullivan, "King Marcus Antonius Polemo," 6–20. Sullivan and Barrett disagreed on many points, but not on the dating of the coinage.

23. Tacitus, *Histories* 5.9; Tacitus, *Annals* 12.54.

24. Josephus, *Jewish War* 2 §§ 254–265; Josephus, *Jewish Antiquities* 20 §§ 160–166.

25. Josephus, *Jewish Antiquities* 20 §§ 179–181.

26. Josephus, *Jewish Antiquities* 20 §§ 182–184.

27. Josephus, *Jewish Antiquities* 19 § 294.

28. Josephus, *Jewish Antiquities* 20 §§ 49–53, and Mishnah Nazir 3:6.

29. See Avigad, "Burial-Vault," 185–200. In regard to the practice, see also Mishnah Nazir 6:11 in its description of Miriam of Palmyra. Chepey, *Nazirites,* 86–89, makes a cogent case for viewing Josephus's characterization of Helena in association with the Mishnaic claim that she was a Nazirite (Mishnah Nazir 3:6). Perhaps, however, her piety came more in the form of the patronage of Nazirites, as in the case of Agrippa I. In the case of the evidence recorded by Avigad, Chepey, *Nazirites,* 71–72, concludes convincingly that Nazirites could belong to the economic elite. Less categorically, Chepey concludes that if one was designated a Nazir in death that meant that one had been a practitioner "of lifelong duration" (also 71–72). I prefer to take the evidence as simply meaning that such a person had a reputation for repeated Nazirite practice, as is attributed to Queen Helena in Mishnah Nazir 3:6.

30. See, for example, 1 Corinthians 16:1–4; 2 Corinthians 8:1–9:15; and Downs, *Offering of the Gentiles.*

31. This is described in the book of Acts 18:18. Stuart Chepey, in his *Nazirites,* 159–164, effectively cuts through the prejudice that has prevented commentators from

acknowledging that the reference is to a Nazirite vow. Absent from his consideration, however, is any evaluation of the positive role that the Temple played in Paul's program. Chepey also assumes that Paul cut his hair in Cenchrea to complete the vow. But the text states that he did so *eiken gar eukhên*, "because he was having a vow." The verb "was having" is in the imperfect form (*eiken*), indicating a continuous state or action, and conveying the thought that Paul's vow conditioned his actions, so that he had his head shaved as part of an enduring process. For this reason, it is more plausible that Paul removed hair from his head so that what was regrown during the next phase of his journey could be offered in Jerusalem. The Temple there was the place to complete a Nazirite vow.

32. Uncharacteristically, Chepey, *Nazirites*, 165–174 convolutes the situation needlessly. Chepey argues, on the basis of a suggestion by Paul Billerbeck, that the four men with James and Paul were indeed in the process of the Nazirite vow, but they all had been subject to "corpse contamination," and therefore had to purify themselves afresh before completing the vow. The scenario envisaged then has them engage in the additional rites set out in Numbers 6:9–12. But the verb that Chepey cites Luke using to refer to purification, the Greek *hagnizô* (Acts 21:24, 26), in fact relates to sanctification, becoming sacred (*hagnos*); see the *Cambridge Greek Lexicon*, 9, 10. That is nothing other than the actual purpose of the Nazirite vow, in which the person involved becomes a source of sanctification, as the name Nazir implies. This sense of the vow is beautifully developed in Diamond, "Israelite Self-Offering in the Priestly Code," 1–18, an article that Chepey does not cite. In the end, Chepey agrees that the Nazirite vow is the point of the practice in Acts 21, but his resort to an extra rite of purification is unnecessarily elaborate. He finds it "easily conceivable" that the incidents of corpse contamination were such that they were "all taking place simultaneously," but I do not find the coincidence easy to imagine. Notably, he also dismisses Jacob Neusner's suggestion that Rabbinic sources do not accord with Luke's presentation, and yet comes himself to the conclusion that actual practice could include "*bending* known rules for the Nazirate" and that the Mishnah represents "*ideal* behaviour" (163, his italics in both cases). That instances an obvious dependency on Neusner's critical advance in the study of the Mishnah and related literature.

33. See Acts 21:27–32; Josephus, *Jewish War* 5 §§ 193–194; Josephus, *Jewish Antiquities* 15 § 417; and Rousseau and Arav, *Jesus and His World*, 312–313.

34. Josephus, *Jewish Antiquities* 20 §§ 173–178, 182–184.

CHAPTER 5. PENITENT IN JERUSALEM

1. Josephus, *Jewish War* 2 § 271; Josephus, *Jewish Antiquities* 20 §§ 185–188.

2. Josephus, *Jewish Antiquities* 20 § 179.

3. Josephus, *Jewish Antiquities* 20 §§ 189–190.

4. Josephus, *Jewish Antiquities* 20 §§ 191–196.

5. Josephus, *Jewish Antiquities* 20 § 195.

6. The dates of Festus's accession and death are matters of uncertainty. The evidence is well set out by Alexis Bunine in "Paul, Jacques, Félix, Festus et les autres," 387–408, 531–562. In this remarkably up-to-date and comprehensive work, the author dates Festus much earlier than most scholars, between 56 and 60 CE, putting James's death in the latter year. The approach also involves bringing Paul to Jerusalem and to Rome earlier than most scholars place those events. The argument turns on indications of traveling conditions in relation to the changing times of year in which feasts were dates. Since those references appear in the story of Paul's journeys by sea in the book of Acts, adventures that are widely considered fictive, taking them to be the basis of historical reconstruction is not recommended. Cf. Troftgruben, "Slow Sailing in Acts," 949–968.

7. Josephus, *Jewish Antiquities* 20 §§ 197–200; Eusebius, *Ecclesiastical History* 2.23. Stuart Chepey, in his *Nazirites*, 174–177, goes out of his way to characterize as legendary the source Eusebius cites in regard to James (Hegesippus), yet he agrees that "Nazirite holiness" within early Christianity was at issue. Since Chepey accepts the references to Nazirite practice in Acts, as discussed earlier, that is a consistent finding.

8. Josephus, *Jewish Antiquities* 17 §§ 299–314.

9. Compare Josephus, *Jewish War* 4 §§ 318–322, with his *Jewish Antiquities* 20 §§ 199–201.

10. Josephus, *Jewish Antiquities* 20 §§ 201–203.

11. Josephus, *Jewish Antiquities* 20 §§ 204–210.

12. Josephus, *Jewish Antiquities* 20 §§ 211–212.

13. This was the suggestion of Grace Harriet Macurdy in *Vassal-Queens*, 84–91, esp. 86. A careful, pioneering work, Macurdy's treatment of Berenice suggests that, given her own analysis of the inscription from the Areopagus, mid-twentieth-century Americans had a bit more difficulty conceiving of Berenice in her own terms than did mid-first-century Athenians.

14. Josephus, *Jewish Antiquities* 20 §§ 213–214, 216–218.

15. Josephus, *Jewish Antiquities* 20 §§ 219–223.

16. Josephus, *Jewish Antiquities* 20 § 215.

17. Josephus, *Jewish Antiquities* 20 §§ 252–258.

18. Tacitus, *Annals* 15.38–44, in *Tacitus*.

19. Josephus, *Life* §§ 13–16, in *Flavius Josephus*.

20. See Braughman, "Poppaea Sabina," 1–18.

21. Suetonius, Nero 35.2, in Suetonius, *Lives of the Caesars*.

22. Florus's actions are described in Josephus, *Jewish War* 2 §§ 277–308, Pilate's in *Jewish War* 2 §§ 175–177.

23. Josephus, *Jewish War* 2 §§ 310–314.

24. See Anagnostou-Laoutides and Charles, "Titus and Berenice," 32–35. Chepey, *Nazirites*, 57–61, finds that Josephus's account of Berenice's Nazirite vow is "the most detailed description of the Nazirite vow in any historical narrative pertaining to the period under study." He also agrees with me that Berenice's appearance in Jerusalem carried associations with rituals of mourning, in particular for thirty days, although he does not discuss the suggestion that James's alternative name in Hegesippus is derived from the Aramaic term for "mourner"; see Chilton, *Resurrection Logic*, 123–132, where earlier literature is cited.

25. Josephus, *Jewish War* 2 §§ 330–332.

26. Josephus, *Jewish War* 2 §§ 333–335.

27. Because both the New Testament and Josephus are kind to Agrippa II, scholarship also has tended to portray him as pious. Kokkinos, *Herodian Dynasty*, 322, claims that "the Herodian king lived almost permanently in Jerusalem." Even if we knew that was generally the case (which would appear odd given his deep ties with Rome), the fate of Jerusalem depended on actions during the period covered by the qualifier "almost." Agrippa II was simply not there at the right time, as Berenice was. As Christian-Georges Schwentzel has remarked in *Hérode le Grand*, 267–269, he was more onlooker and enabler than participant.

28. Josephus, *Jewish War* 2 §§ 336–338.

29. Josephus, *Jewish War* 2 §§ 339–404.

30. Josephus, *Jewish War* 2 §§ 405–407.

31. Josephus, *Jewish War* 2 §§ 408–432.

32. Josephus, *Jewish War* 2 §§ 494–497.

33. Josephus, *Jewish War* 2 §§ 499–594.

34. Josephus, *Jewish War* 2 §§ 632–646.

35. Josephus, *Life* §§ 64–67.

36. Suetonius, Nero 28.1; Dio Cassius, *Roman History* 62.28.2; Plutarch, Life of Galba 9, in Plutarch, *Lives*.

37. Suetonius, Vespasian 4.4, in Suetonius, *Lives of the Caesars*.

38. Josephus, *Jewish War* 3 §§ 141–391, esp. §§ 350–354 (with further context in §§ 110–114, 129–140). In Josephus's conception, Latin *fortuna* (*tuche* in Josephus's

Greek) and the Septuagint's *pronoia* operated together to make the Roman victory a providential necessity. For an analysis along these lines, see Kelley, "Cosmopolitan Expression," 257–274. She provides an incisive analysis of the presentations of the closing events of the siege at Jotapata and the famous siege at Masada. Josephus's detailed description of the siege and the tactics deployed on both sides remain convincing (apart from sporadic claims of Roman discomfiture and Josephan heroism), however self-interested and theologically argumentative it is. Still, when he claims that all Jerusalem went into mourning at the report of his death (*Jewish War* 3 § 436), the effect is inadvertently comic.

39. Josephus, *Jewish War* 3 §§ 392–408; Tacitus, *History* 5.13; cf. Suetonius, Vespasian 4.5.

40. Josephus, *Jewish War* 3 §§ 443–445.

41. Josephus, *Jewish War* 3 §§ 445–542.

42. Plutarch, Life of Galba 4–5.

CHAPTER 6. TITUS'S PARAMOUR IN ROME

1. See Josephus, *Jewish Antiquities* 20 §§ 143–145.

2. Tacitus, *Annals,* 15.48–74, in *Tacitus.*

3. Conditions in Jerusalem are described in Josephus, *Jewish War* 4 §§ 410–413, and Vespasian's posture in *Jewish War* 4 §§ 366–376, 440–450, 486–490.

4. Tacitus, *Histories* 1.1–2.1, in *Tacitus.*

5. Suetonius, Otho 3.1–2, in Suetonius, *Lives of the Caesars;* Plutarch, Life of Galba 19–20, in Plutarch, *Lives;* Josephus, *Jewish War* 4 §§ 491–502.

6. Compare Tacitus, *Histories* 2.1, with Josephus, *Jewish War* 4 § 501.

7. Tacitus, *Histories* 2.5, 74. The importance of Mucianus is the special concern of John Crook in his "Titus and Berenice." By tracing Mucianus's relationship to Titus, Crook offers a sensible account of Roman politics in regard to Titus's accession and the challenge posed by Berenice's ambition.

8. Josephus deals in *Jewish War* both with Vespasian's continuing tactics (4 §§ 545–555) and with his learning news from Rome (4 §§ 585–591).

9. Josephus, *Jewish War* 4 §§ 592–600.

10. Tacitus, *Histories* 2.5, 74–85.

11. Tacitus, *Histories* 1.15.

12. Tacitus, *Histories* 2.6–7, 74–78.

13. Josephus, *Jewish War* 3 §§ 70–109.

14. Tacitus, *Histories* 2.81.

15. Tacitus, *Histories* 3.65; Suetonius, Vespasian 4.3, in Suetonius, *Lives of the Caesars*.

16. Josephus, *Jewish War* 4 §§ 601–663.

17. Tacitus, *Histories* 3.48.

18. Josephus, *Jewish War* 4 §§ 616–617.

19. Tacitus, *Histories* 2.79.

20. Josephus, *Jewish War* 5 §§ 39–46.

21. Tacitus, *Histories* 1.10; 2.1; 4.81–82; 5.13; Josephus, *Jewish War* 6 §§ 312–315; Dio Cassius, *Roman History* 66.1; Suetonius, Vespasian 4.5–5.7; 7.1–3; 25.

22. Tacitus, *Histories* 4.51–52; Suetonius, Domitian 1.3, in Suetonius, *Lives of the Caesars*.

23. Josephus, *Jewish War* 5 §§ 491–501; Tacitus, *Histories* 5.1, 11.

24. Josephus, *Jewish War* 5 § 47–6 § 442, for his to some extent eyewitness description, and 5 §§ 362–419 for his self-portrayal.

25. Josephus, *Jewish War* 5 §§ 541–547.

26. Josephus, *Jewish War* 5 §§ 446–451.

27. These improbable claims punctuate Josephus's narrative; see *Jewish War* 5 §§ 455–456, 522; 6 §§ 214–219.

28. For Titus's alleged orders concerning the Temple, see Josephus, *Jewish War* 6 §§ 93–128.

29. For this climax, see especially Josephus, *Jewish War* 6 §§ 164–168, 177–186, 191–192, 228.

30. The denouement comes in Josephus, *Jewish War* 6 §§ 232–243, 249–266.

31. For Titus's apologia, see Josephus, *Jewish War* 6 §§ 323–350, 409–413. Josephus's estimate of casualties appears in *Jewish War* 6 §§ 414–420.

32. These arrangements, including the grisly afterparty, are described in Josephus, *Jewish War* 7 §§ 1–24.

33. See Dio Cassius, *Roman History* 65.15, and Josephus, *Jewish War* 7 §§ 116–157.

34. His *Life* appears in Josephus (Flavius), *The Life. Against Apion.*

35. In his *Life,* Josephus refers to Berenice's intervention on behalf of Justus in §§ 343, 355–356. He writes of her wealth in wheat in *Life* §§ 118–119, and possibly alludes to Agrippa II's death in *Life* § 359.

36. See Quintilian, *Orator's Education* 4.1.19; Young-Widmaier, "Quintilian's Legal Representation of Julia Berenice," 124–129; Braund, "Berenice in Rome," 120–123; Rogers, "Titus, Berenice, and Mucianus," 86–95; and Vasta, "Titus and the Queen."

37. See Dio Cassius, *Roman History* 65.15; in regard to the honor, see Philo, *Against Flaccus* § 40, in *Philo,* and Rémy, "Ornati et ornamenta quaestoria," 160–198.

38. This is the opinion of most scholars, against the picture of Ruth Jordan, who depicts Berenice and Titus as a new edition of Cleopatra and Antony; see Jordan, *Berenice,* 206. She also depicts Berenice as flaunting her sexual relationship with Agrippa (103).

39. It is interesting that the expression of hope precedes the description; cf. Josephus, *Jewish War* 5 §§ 184–247 and § 19.

40. Referenced in Josephus, *Jewish War* 7 §§ 158–162. Some of them are still visible today in the depiction on the Arch of Titus.

41. See Suetonius, Titus 6.1–2, and *Epitome de Caesaribus* § 10.4, both in Suetonius, *Lives of the Caesars*. An argument for a later dating of the *Epitome,* after the middle of the sixth century CE, is mounted by Stover and Woudhuysen in "Jordanes and the Date of the *Epitome de Caesaribus,*" 150–188. At the same time, they detail arguments for an earlier dating (usually a century earlier), and set out a cogent case for the *Epitome*'s recourse to still earlier material.

42. See Suetonius, Titus 7.2; Vergil, *Aeneid* 6.460 in *Virgil;* and Smallwood, *Jews Under Roman Rule,* 387–388. Despite making a connection between Aeneas and Dido and Titus and Berenice, Smallwood also invokes the standard comparison with Cleopatra, "with the temptress not luring the Roman to the East but trying to establish herself in Rome" (387). Throughout, she minimizes Titus's affection for Berenice and the amount of time that Berenice spent in Rome (all the while, it must be acknowledged, calling attention to the thinness of the evidence). Neither of those maneuvers makes sense of the problem that Titus evidently had to acknowledge by agreeing to part from Berenice, or of his notorious violence in defense of her prior to that moment. Smallwood's comparison with *Aeneid* is much more to the point. In this regard, it is notable that discussion after her time found that Vergil's allusions included Berenice II, the Ptolemaic queen; see Johnston, "Dido, Berenice, and Arsinoe," 649–654. Might Suetonius have been aware of the connection? In that case, his famous use of *invitus, invitam* might have expressed an unexpected degree of sympathy for Berenice. See also MacRae, "*Invitus invitam,*" 415–418.

43. Suetonius, Titus 7.1–2.

44. Suetonius, Vespasian 24.

45. Josephus, *Jewish Antiquities* 20 § 144. The reference to this son as perishing

"with the woman" seems to me to refer more naturally to Drusilla than to an unnamed and otherwise unmentioned wife.

46. Dio Cassius, *Roman History* 66.18.1, relates the visit, and 66.24–26 describes Titus's exertions.

47. Suetonius, Titus 11.

EPILOGUE

1. Suetonius, Domitian 2, in Suetonius, *Lives of the Caesars.*

2. Some of Revelation's imagery (for example, 13:11–18; 17:9–14) and specific complaint (6:5–6) may be read in terms of Suetonius, Domitian 7.2; 12.2; 14:2.

3. The events are detailed in Collins, "Palace Revolution," 73–106. As a matter of policy, Domitian distanced himself from the Herodians, except in one interesting area: hunting. His use of hunting as a projection of power has been a topic of investigation; see Tuck, "Origins of Roman Imperial Hunting Imagery," 221–245. Herod the Great's prowess in this regard is vaunted by Josephus (see, for example, Josephus, *Jewish War* 1 §§ 429–430). Herodian propaganda of the hunt may have influenced Domitian by means of Josephus.

4. Suetonius, Titus 7.1, in Suetonius, *Lives of the Caesars.*

5. See Tacitus, *Histories* 2.2, in *Tacitus,* and Dio Cassius, *Roman History* 65.15.

6. See Josephus, *Jewish Antiquities* 20 §§ 143, 145, and Dio Cassius, *Roman History* 60.8.5.

7. Josephus, *Life* §§ 343, 355–356, in *Flavius Josephus.*

8. Macurdy, *Vassal-Queens,* 86–91. Ruth Jordan, by contrast, makes this claim the centerpiece of her biography.

9. See Scudéry, "Bérénice à Titus." For discussion see Denis and Spica, *Madeleine de Scudéry.*

10. This and subsequent quotations in this paragraph are translated from Scudéry, "Bérénice à Titus," 152, 156, 167–168.

11. Influences on Racine and his extraordinary impact are discussed in Akerman, *Mythe de Bérénice.* See also Jasinski, "Trois sujets raciniens avant Racine," 2–56. Racine's rivalry with Corneille is explored in Defaux, "Case of Bérénice," 211–239.

12. These are lines 1499–1500 in the 1671 edition (Paris: Barbin), in a text established by Paul Fièvre in 2023 for *Théâtre Classique.* The earlier example consists of the broken lines prior to 625. I refer to this edition in what follows, since the enumeration of lines allows precision, but also indicate the acts and scenes for those using other

editions. For Titus's relationship to Bérénice, see Evans, "Does Titus Really Love Bérénice?," 454–458.

13. Racine in the Fièvre edition, l. 624 (II iv).

14. Racine in the Fièvre edition, ll. 446, 459 (II ii).

15. Racine in the Fièvre edition, ll. 585–588 (II iv), 769–770 (III i).

16. Racine in the Fièvre edition, ll. 1024–1026 (IV iv), 1420–1425 (V vi).

17. Racine carefully plots Bérénice's expression of confidence, ll. 151–177 (I iv), her condescension, ll. 259–261 (I iv), and her refusal to heed warnings, ll. 295–326 (I v).

18. Compare their assertions in ll. 529–530 (II ii) and ll. 575–577 (II iv) in the Fièvre edition.

19. Racine in the Fièvre edition, ll. 665–666 (II v).

20. Racine in the Fièvre edition, ll. 907–911 (III iii).

21. This sequence of steps builds in the Fièvre edition, l. 1063; ll. 1126–1129; and ll. 1186, 1188–1190 (IV v).

22. Racine in the Fièvre edition, l. 1334 (V v) and ll. 1481–1482 (V scène dernière).

23. The 2000 production of *Bérénice,* directed by Jean-Daniel Verhaeghe with Gérard Depardieu in the role of Titus (https://www.imdb.com/title/tt0255858/), a film made for television, fortunately can still be viewed. Bouquet recently returned to the role; see Palou, "Carole Bouquet." In an interview for the latest production in which she played the lead, Bouquet remarked that the play turns on the issue of "rénoncement"; see Dalmaz, "'C'est Racine que me fascine, beaucoup plus que Bérénice.'" T. S. Eliot came to the same conclusion in regard to renunciation as a grounding concern of *Bérénice;* see Gervais, "T. S. Eliot and Racine," 51–70.

24. Racine in the Fièvre edition, ll. 384–396, 426–430 (II ii).

25. Voltaire's dismissal of Corneille's play as among the worst in the history of French theater is often discussed; Hammond, "Corneille," 278–295. See Schlieper, "Helden-Geschlechter," 53–96, and Labrune, "Trois cent cinquante ans de concurrence."

26. Levin, *Last Ember,* 6. Dan Brown's *Da Vinci Code* was published in 2003 by Doubleday.

27. The site IMDb provides details about the series at https://www.imdb.com/title/tt10569934/. The series is based on a book by Daniel P. Mannix, which also inspired the film *Gladiator*.

28. See Atwill, *Caesar's Messiah,* 2, 5, 255. A similarly strained theory, pressed in a different direction, makes Berenice the model for the deuterocanonical book of Judith; see Mireaux, *La Reine Bérénice*. Attempts at revisionism often fall at the first hurdle of chronology.

29. Moussaieff, "'New Cleopatra,'" 47–49.

30. Akerman, *Mythe de Bérénice;* Goorah-Martin, "À la recherche de l'origine du mythe de Bérénice." Goorah-Martin's study offers a particularly interesting investigation into how, in modern mythology, the Herodian Berenice has been welded together with Egyptian Berenices.

31. Collingwood, *Principles of History,* 30. Collingwood develops this principle within a discussion of a hypothetical detective story; Berenice's incest is perhaps a clearer case.

32. Collingwood, *Autobiography,* 114.

33. Tacitus, *Annals,* 13.7, 14.26, in *Tacitus.*

34. Josephus, *Jewish Antiquities* 18 §§ 139–141. Josephus describes this branch of the family as having left aside Judaic practice in favor of Greek customs.

35. Josephus, *Jewish Antiquities* 18 §§ 127–128.

36. Ilan, *Queen Berenice,* 177–184, and Segni, "On a Dated Inscription," 277–280.

37. See Drijvers, "Ammianus Marcellinus 23.1.2–3."

38. See, for example, Feldman, "Jewish Theocracy," 431–452.

39. The letter is numbered 51 in Julian, *Letters. Epigrams.*

40. Freeman, *Julian.*

41. Suetonius, Titus 8.1.

Bibliography

ANCIENT SOURCES

Babylonian Talmud Hebrew-English Edition. 30 vols. Ed. Isidore Epstein. London: Soncino, 1965–1989.

Corpus Papyrorum Judaicorum. 3 vols. Ed. Victor Tcherikover, Alexander Fuks, and Menahem Stern. Cambridge: Harvard University Press, 1957–1964.

Dio Cassius. *Roman History.* 9 vols. Loeb Classical Library 32, 37, 53, 66, 82–83, 175–177. Ed. and trans. Earnest Cary and Herbert B. Foster. Cambridge: Harvard University Press, 1914–1927.

Epitome de Caesaribus. Canisius College Translated Texts 1. Ed. and trans. Thomas M. Banchich. Buffalo, N.Y.: Canisius College, 2018.

Eusebius. *Ecclesiastical History.* 2 vols. Loeb Classical Library 153, 265. Ed. and trans. Kirsopp Lake and John Ernest Leonard Oulton. Cambridge: Harvard University Press, 1930–1932.

Flavius Josephus: Translation and Commentary. Ed. Steve Mason. Leiden: Brill, 1999–2024.

Josephus (Flavius). *Jewish Antiquities.* 9 vols. Loeb Classical Library 242, 281, 326, 365, 410, 433, 456, 489, 490. Ed. and trans. Hector St. J. Thackeray, Ralph Marcus, Allen Wikgren, and Louis H. Feldman. Cambridge: Harvard University Press, 1970–2000.

Josephus (Flavius). *The Jewish War.* 3 vols. Loeb Classical Library 203, 210, 487. Ed. and trans. Hector St. J. Thackeray. Cambridge: Harvard University Press, 1927–1928.

Josephus (Flavius). *The Life. Against Apion.* Loeb Classical Library 186. Ed. and trans. Hector St. J. Thackeray. Cambridge: Harvard University Press, 1926.

Julian. *Letters. Epigrams. Against the Galilaeans. Fragments.* Loeb Classical Library 157. Ed. and trans. Wilmer C. Wright. Cambridge: Harvard University Press, 1923.

Juvenal and Perseus. Loeb Classical Library 91. Ed. and trans. Susanna Morton Braund. Cambridge: Harvard University Press, 1928.

Mishnayoth. 7 vols. Ed. and trans. Philip Blackman. Gateshead, U.K.: Judaica Press, 1963–1964.

Bibliography

Novum Testamentum Graece. Ed. Barbara Aland, Kurt Aland, et al. Stuttgart: Deutsche Bibelgesellschaft, 2012.

Philo. 10 vols. Loeb Classical Library 226, 227, 247, 261, 275, 289, 320, 341, 363, 379. Ed. and trans. Francis H. Colson and George H. Whitaker. Cambridge: Harvard University Press, 1929–1967.

Photius. Bibliothèque (Codices 230–241). Collection Byzantine. Ed. and trans. René Henry. Paris: Belles Lettres, 1967.

Plato in Twelve Volumes. Vol. 9. Trans. W. R. M. Lamb. Cambridge: Harvard University Press, 1925.

Plutarch. *Lives*. 11 vols. Loeb Classical Library 46–47, 65, 80, 87, 98–103. Ed. and trans. Bernadotte Perrin. Cambridge: Harvard University Press, 1914–1926.

Quintilian. *The Orator's Education*. Loeb Classical Library 124–127, 494. Ed. and trans. Donald A. Russell. Cambridge: Harvard University Press, 2001.

Select Papyri. 3 vols. Loeb Classical Library 266, 282, 360. Ed. and trans. Arthur Surridge Hunt, Campbell Cowan Edgar, and Denys Lionel Page. Cambridge: Harvard University Press, 1932.

Suetonius. *Lives of the Caesars*. 2 vols. Loeb Classical Library 31, 38. Ed. and trans. John Carew Rolfe. Cambridge: Harvard University Press, 1914.

Tacitus. 5 vols. Loeb Classical Library 35, 111, 249, 312, 322. Ed. and trans. Eric Herbert Warmington, Maurice Hutton, John Jackson, Clifford Hershel Moore, R. M. Ogilvie, William Peterson, and Michael Winterbottom. Cambridge: Harvard University Press, 1980–1992.

Virgil. 2 vols. Loeb Classical Library 63–64. Ed. and trans. H. Rushton Fairclough. Cambridge: Harvard University Press, 1934–1935. Reprint, 1998.

MODERN SOURCES

Ager, Sheila L. "Marriage or Mirage? The Phantom Wedding of Cleopatra and Antony." *Classical Philology* 108, no. 2 (2013).

Akerman, Simone. *Le Mythe de Bérénice*. Paris: Nizet, 1978.

Anagnostou-Laoutides, Eva, and Michael B. Charles. "Titus and Berenice: The Elegaic Aura of an Historical Affair." *Arethusa* 48 (2015): 17–46.

Appelbaum, Alan. "On the Apostasy of Tiberius Julius Alexander." *Journal of Ancient Judaism* 14, no. 1 (2023).

Atwill, Joseph. *Caesar's Messiah: The Roman Conspiracy to Invent Jesus*. Berkeley, Calif.: Ulysses, 2005.

Bibliography

Avigad, Nahman. "The Burial-Vault of a Nazirite Family on Mount Scopus." *Israel Exploration* 21, no. 4 (1971).

Barrett, Anthony A. "Polemo II of Pontus and M. Antonius Polemo." *Zeitschrift für Alte Geshichte* 27, no. 3 (1978).

Berthelot, Katell. "*The Rabbis Write Back!* L'enjeu de la 'parenté' entre Israël et Rome-Ésaü-Édom." *Revue de l'histoire des religions* 233, no. 2 (2016).

Blanton, Thomas R., IV. "The Expressive Prepuce: Philo's Defense of Judaic Circumcision in Greek and Roman Contexts." *Studia Philonica Annual* 31 (2019).

Braughman, Karl E. "Poppaea Sabina, Jewish Sympathies, and the Fire of Rome." *Women in Judaism* 11, no. 2 (2014).

Braund, D. C. "Berenice in Rome." *Historia* 33, no. 1 (1984): 120–123.

Brewer, David Instone. "Jewish Women Divorcing Their Husbands in Early Judaism: The Background to Papyrus Ṣe'elim 13." *Harvard Theological Review* 92, no. 3 (1999).

Brooten, Bernadette. "Könnten Frauen im alten Judentum die Scheidung betreiben? Überlegung zu Mk 10, 11–12 und 1Kor 7, 10–11." *Evangelische Theologie* 42 (1982).

Bunine, Alexis. "Paul, Jacques, Félix, Festus et les autres: Pour un revision de la chronologie des derniers procurateurs de Palestine." *Revue Biblique* 111, nos. 3–4 (2004).

Cambridge Greek Lexicon, The. Ed. James Diggle. Cambridge: Cambridge University Press, 2021.

Chapman, Honora Howell, and Zuleika Rodgers, eds. *A Companion to Josephus.* Chichester, U.K.: Wiley Blackwell, 2016.

Chepey, Stuart. *Nazirites in Late Second Temple Judaism: A Survey of Ancient Jewish Writings, the New Testament, Archaeological Evidence, and Other Writings from Late Antiquity.* Leiden: Brill, 2005.

Chilton, Bruce. *The Herods: Murder, Politics, and the Art of Succession.* Minneapolis: Fortress, 2021.

Chilton, Bruce. *Rabbi Paul: An Intellectual Biography.* New York: Doubleday, 2004.

Chilton, Bruce. *Resurrection Logic: How Jesus' First Followers Believed God Raised Him from the Dead.* Waco, Tex.: Baylor University Press, 2019.

Collingwood, Robin G. *Autobiography*. London: Oxford University Press, 1939.

Collingwood, Robin G. *The Principles of Art.* Oxford: Clarendon, 1938.

Collingwood, Robin G. *The Principles of History and Other Writings in Philosophy of*

History. Ed. W. H. Dray and W. J. van der Dussen. Oxford: Oxford University Press, 1999.

Collins, Andrew W. "The Palace Revolution: The Assassination of Domitian and the Accession of Nerva." *Phoenix* 63, nos. 1–2 (2009).

Crook, John A. "Titus and Berenice." *American Journal of Philology* 72 (1951): 162–175.

Dalmaz, Véronique. "'C'est Racine que me fascine, beaucoup plus que Bérénice': Carole Bouquet sur scène à Nice dans une version moderne d'une des plus grandes tragedies." *FranceInfo,* October 4, 2023.

Defaux, Gérard. "The Case of Bérénice: Racine, Corneille, and Mimetic Desire." Trans. Michael Metteer. *Yale French Studies* 76 (1989).

Denis, Delphine, and Anne Élisabeth Spica, eds. *Madeleine de Scudéry. Une femme de lettres aux XVII siècle: Études littéraires.* Arras, Fr.: Artois Presses Université, 2002.

Diamond, Eliezer. "An Israelite Self-Offering in the Priestly Code: A New Perspective on the Nazirite." *Jewish Quarterly Review* 88, nos. 1–2 (1997).

Downs, David J. *The Offering of the Gentiles: Paul's Collection for Jerusalem in Its Chronological, Cultural, and Cultic Contexts.* Tübingen: Mohr Siebeck, 2008.

Drijvers, Jan Willem. "Ammianus Marcellinus 23.1.2–3: The Rebuilding of the Temple in Jerusalem." Pp. 19–26 in J. den Boeft, Daniel den Hengst, and H. C. Teitler, eds., *Cognitio Gestorum. The Historiographic Art of Ammianus Marcellinus.* Amsterdam: North-Holland, 1992.

Endres, John C. *Biblical Interpretation in the Book of Jubilees.* Washington, D.C.: Catholic Biblical Association of America, 1997.

Evans, Katherine. "Alexander the Alabarch: Roman and Jew." In *Society of Biblical Literature. 1995 Seminar Papers.* Ed. Eugene H. Lovering, Jr. Atlanta: Scholars Press, 1995.

Evans, William M. "Does Titus Really Love Bérénice?" *Romance Notes* 15, no. 3 (1974).

Feldman, Rachel Z. "Jewish Theocracy at the Biblical Barbeque: The Role of Third Temple Activism and Sacrificial Reenactments in Shaping Self and State." *Contemporary Jewry* 40, no. 3 (2020).

Fièvre, Paul. *Bérénice: Tragédie. Par M. Racine.* Rev. November 2016. *Théâtre Classique* online editions. Available at https://theatre-classique.fr/pages/programmes/edition.php?t=../documents/RACINE_BERENICE.xml.

Fine, Steven, ed. *The Temple of Jerusalem: From Moses to the Messiah.* Leiden: Brill, 2011.

Freeman, Philip. *Julian: Rome's Last Pagan Emperor.* New Haven: Yale University Press, 2023.

Freisenbruch, Annelise. "Little Cleopatra: A Jewish Princess and the First Ladies of the Flavian Dynasty." Pp. 133–154 in Freisenbruch, *Caesars' Wives: Sex, Power, and Politics in the Roman Empire*. New York: Free Press, 2010.

Friedland, Elise A. *The Roman Marble Sculptures from the Sanctuary of Pan at Caesarea Philippi/Panias (Israel)*. Boston: American Schools of Oriental Research, 2012.

Fuks, Alexander. "Marcus Julius Alexander." *Zion* 13 (1944).

Gambetti, Sandra. *The Alexandrian Riots of 38 C.E. and the Persecution of the Jews: A Historical Reconstruction*. Leiden: Brill, 2009.

Geagan, Daniel J. "Tiberius Claudius Novius, the Hoplite Generalship and Epimeleteia of the Free City of Athens." *American Journal of Philology* 100, no. 2 (1979).

Gervais, David. "T. S. Eliot and Racine: Tragedy and Resignation in *Bérénice*." *Cambridge Quarterly* 36, no. 1 (2007).

Goodman, Martin. *Herod the Great: Jewish King in a Roman World*. New Haven: Yale University Press, 2024.

Goorah-Martin, Annie. "À la recherche de l'origine du mythe de Bérénice." M.A. thesis, McGill University, 1996.

Hammond, Paul. "Corneille: *Tite et Bérénice*." Pp. 278–295 in Hammond, *Tragic Agency in Classical Drama from Aeschylus to Voltaire*. Leiden: Brill, 2021.

Hayes, Christine. "Intermarriage and Impurity in Ancient Jewish Sources." *Harvard Theological Review* 92, no. 1 (1999): 3–36.

Hirschman, Jan V., Peter Richardson, Ross S. Kraemer, and Philip A. Mackowiak. "Death of an Arabian Jew." *Archives of Internal Medicine* 164, no. 8 (2003).

Ilan, Tal. *Queen Berenice. A Jewish Female Icon of the First Century CE*. Leiden: Brill, 2022.

Jacobson, David M. *Agrippa II. The Last of the Herods*. Routledge Biographies. London: Routledge, 2019.

Jacobson, David M. "Coins of the First Century Roman Governors of Judaea and Their Motifs." *Electrum* 26 (2019).

Jasinski, René. "Trois sujets raciniens avant Racine." *Revue d'Histoire littéraire de la France* 47, no. 1 (1947).

Johnson, Peter. "R. G. Collingwood on Biography: A Reconsideration." *Collingwood and British Idealism Studies* 23, no. 7 (2017).

Johnston, Patricia A. "Dido, Berenice, and Arsinoe: *Aeneid* 6.460." *American Journal of Philology* 108, no. 4 (1987).

Jordan, Ruth. *Berenice*. London: Constable, 1974.

Bibliography

Kelley, Nicole. "The Cosmopolitan Expression of Josephus's Prophetic Perspective in the 'Jewish War.'" *Harvard Theological Review* 97, no. 3 (2004).

Kindler, Arie. "A Coin of Herod Philip—The Earliest Portrait of a Herodian Ruler." *Israel Exploration Journal* 21, nos. 2–3 (1971).

Kirchner, Johannes, ed. *Inscriptiones Graecae II et III: Inscriptiones Atticae Euclidis anno posteriors I–III*. Berlin: Berlin-Brandenburgischen Akademie der Wissenschaften, 1913–1940.

Kokkinos, Nikos. *Antonia Augusta: Portrait of a Great Roman Lady*. London: Libri, 2002.

Kokkinos, Nikos. *The Herodian Dynasty: Origins, Role in Society and Eclipse*. Sheffield, U.K.: Sheffield Academic Press, 1998.

Krieger, Klaus-Stefan. "Berenike—Die Schwester König Aggripas II., bei Flavius Josephus." *Journal for the Study of Judaism* 28 (1997): 1–11.

Kropp, Andreas J. M. "Crowning the Emperor: An Unorthodox Image of Claudius, Agrippa I and Herod of Chalkis," *Syria* 90 (2013).

Kultermann, Udo. "The 'Dance of the Seven Veils': Salome and Erotic Culture around 1900," *Artibus et Historiae* 27, no. 53 (2003).

Labrune, Caroline. "Trois cent cinquante ans de concurrence: Les *Bérénice*, du duel officiel au verdict implicite." *Epistémè* 40 (2021). https://journals.openedition.org/episteme/13685.

Ladouceur, David J. "The Death of Herod the Great," *Classical Philology* 76, no. 1 (1981).

Lange, Carsten Hort, and Jesper Majbom Madsen, eds. *Cassius Dio: Greek Intellectual and Roman Politician*. Historiography of Rome and Its Empire. Leiden: Brill, 2016.

Leslie, Stephen W. and Juron Foreman. "Fournier Gangrene." *National Library of Medicine*, February 15, 2025. https://www.ncbi.nlm.nih.gov/books/NBK549821/.

Levick, Barbara. "Titus and the Jewish Princess." *Wolfson College, Oxford: College Record* (1999–2000): 60–73.

Levin, Daniel. *The Last Ember*. New York: Riverhead, 2009.

MacRae, Duncan E. "*Invitus invitam:* A Window Allusion in Suetonius' *Titus*." *Classical Quarterly* 65, no. 1 (2015).

Macurdy, Grace Harriet. "Julia Berenice." *American Journal of Philology* 56, no. 3 (1935): 246–253.

Macurdy, Grace Harriet. *Vassal-Queens and Some Contemporary Women in the Roman Empire*. Baltimore: Johns Hopkins University Press, 1937.

Madden, F. W. *Coins of the Jews*. London: Trübner, 1881.

Bibliography

Martens, John W. *One God, One Law: Philo of Alexandria on the Mosaic and Greco-Roman Law.* Leiden: Brill, 2003.

Mason, Steve. *A History of the Jewish War: AD 66–74.* Cambridge: Cambridge University Press, 2016.

Meshorer, Ya'akov. *A Treasury of Jewish Coins from the Persian Period to Bar Kokhba.* Jerusalem: Yad Ben Zvi, 2001.

Mireaux, Émile. *La Reine Bérénice.* Paris: 1951.

Mommsen, Theodor. *Römische Geschichte.* Berlin: Weidmann, 1927.

Moussaieff, Shlomo. "The 'New Cleopatra' and the Jewish Tax." *Biblical Archaeology Review* 36, no. 1 (2010).

Nasrallah, Laura. "The Acts of the Apostles, Greek Cities, and Hadrian's Panhellion." *Journal of Biblical Literature* 127, no. 3 (2008).

Palou, Anthony. "Carole Bouquet: 'Bérénice c'est un cadeau.'" *Le Figaro,* September 14, 2022.

Power, Tristan, and Roy K. Gibson, eds. *Suetonius the Biographer.* Oxford: Oxford University Press, 2018.

Racine, Jean-Baptiste. *Bérénice: Tragédie.* Paris: Claude Barbin, 1671.

Regev, Eyal. "Herod's Jewish Ideology Facing Romanization: On Intermarriage, Ritual Baths, and Speeches." *Jewish Quarterly Review* 100, no. 2 (2010): 197–222.

Reinach, Théodore, and George Francis Hill. *Jewish Coins.* Trans. Mary Hill. London: Lawrence and Bullen, 1903.

Rémy, Bernard. "Ornati et ornamenta quaestoria, praetoria et consularia sous le haut empire romain." *Revue des Études Anciennes* 78–79, nos. 1–4 (1976–1977).

Roddaz, Jean-Michel. *Marcus Agrippa.* Rome: École française de Rome, 1984.

Rogers, Perry M. "Titus, Berenice, and Mucianus." *Historia* 29, no. 1 (1980): 86–95.

Rosenblum, Jordan D. "'Why Do You Refuse to Eat Pork?' Jews, Food, and Identity in Roman Palestine." *Jewish Quarterly Review* 100, no. 1 (2010): 95–110.

Rousseau, John J., and Rami Arav. *Jesus and His World: An Archaeological and Cultural Dictionary.* Minneapolis: Fortress, 1995.

Schalit, Abraham. *König Herodes. Der Mann und sein Werk.* 1969; Berlin: de Gruyter, 2001.

Schellenberg, Ryan S. "The First Pauline Chronologist? Paul's Itinerary in the Letters and in Acts." *Journal of Biblical Literature* 134, no. 1 (2015).

Schlieper, Hendrik. "Helden-Geschlechter: Die Bérénice-Tragödien Corneilles und

Racines." In *Gattung und Geschlecht: Konventionen und Transformationen eines Paradigmas: Cultura 21,* ed. Hendrik Schleiper and Merle Tönnius. Wiesbaden, Ger.: Harrassowitz, 2021.

Schmalz, Geoffrey C. R. *Augustan and Julio-Claudian Athens: A New Epigraphy and Prosopography.* Leiden: Brill, 2009.

Schürer, Emil. *The History of the Jewish People in the Age of Jesus Christ: A New Revised English Version.* Vol. 1. Ed. Geza Vermes and Ferus Millar. Edinburgh: T. & T. Clark, 1987.

Schwartz, Daniel R. *Agrippa I. The Last King of Judea.* Tübingen: Mohr, 1990.

Schwartz, Daniel R. "*Kata Touton ton Kairon;* Josephus' Source on Agrippa II." *Jewish Quarterly Review* 72 (1982): 241–268.

Schwartz, Daniel R. "On Abraham Schalit, Herod, Josephus, the Holocaust, Horst R. Moehring, and the Study of Ancient Jewish History." *Jewish History* 2, no. 2 (1987).

Schwentzel, Christian-Georges. *Hérode le Grand.* Paris: Pygmalion, 2011.

Scudéry, Madeleine de. "Bérénice à Titus." In *Les Femmes illustres, ou Les Harangues héroïques de Monsieur de Scudéry: Avec les véritables Portraits de ces Héroïnes, tirez des Médailles Antiques.* Paris: Antoine de Sommaville and Augustin Courbé, 1642.

Segni, Leah di. "On a Dated Inscription from Rakhle and the Eras Used on the Hermon Range." *Zeitschrift für Papyrologie und Epigraphik* 117 (1997).

Smallwood, E. Mary. *The Jews Under Roman Rule. From Pompey to Diocletian.* Leiden: Brill, 1976.

Stover, Justin A., and George Woudhuysen. "Jordanes and the Date of the *Epitome de Caesaribus.*" *Histos* 15 (2021).

Sullivan, Richard D. "King Marcus Antonius Polemo." *Numismatic Chronicle* 19 [139] (1979).

Tcherikover, Victor, and Alexander Fuks, eds. *Corpus Papyorum Judaicorum.* Vol. 2. Cambridge: Harvard University Press, 1960.

Treadgold, Warren. *The Nature of the Bibliotheca of Photius.* Dumbarton Oaks Studies. Washington, D.C.: Dumbarton Oaks Center, 1980.

Troftgruben, Troy M. "Slow Sailing in Acts: Suspense in the Final Sea Journey (Acts 27:1–28:15)." *Journal of Biblical Literature* 136, no. 4 (2017).

Tuck, Steven L. "The Origins of Roman Imperial Hunting Imagery: Domitian and the Redefinition of *Virtus* under the Principate." *Greece & Rome* 52, no. 2 (2005).

Vasta, Michael S. "Titus and the Queen: Julia Berenice and the Opposition to Titus' Succession." Honors project paper. Bloomington: Illinois Wesleyan University, 2007. https://digitalcommons.iwu.edu/grs_honproj/1/.

Wardle, David. "Suetonius on Vespasian's Rise to Power Under the Julio-Claudians." *Acta Classica* 53 (2010).

Wasserstein, Abraham, and David J. Wasserstein. *The Legend of the Septuagint: From Classical Antiquity to Today.* Cambridge: Cambridge University Press, 2006.

Watson, Patricia. "The Flight of Pudicitia: Juvenal's Vision of the Past and the Programmatic Function of the Prologue in the Sixth Satire." *Mnemosyne* 65, no. 1 (2012): 62–79.

Wilker, Julia. *Für Rom und Jerusalem. Die herodianische Dynastie im 1. Jahrhundert n. Chr.* Frankfurt am Main: Verlag Antike, 2007.

Wilson, John Francis. *Caesarea Philippi. Banias, the Lost City of Pan.* London: Tauris, 2004.

Woodman, Anthony J. ed. *The Cambridge Companion to Tacitus.* Cambridge: Cambridge University Press, 2009.

Young-Widmaier, Michael R. "Quintilian's Legal Representation of Julia Berenice." *Historia* 51, no. 1 (2002).

Acknowledgments

John Crook, whom I met at St. John's College, Cambridge, in 1974, piqued my interest in Berenice. A classicist and acknowledged expert in Roman law and history, he took a broad interest in other pursuits in the college as its president. He even conversed with me, a newly arrived research student in divinity. Early in his career he wrote on Berenice, and in the process not only showed how Judaic sources, Roman sources, and the New Testament sometimes dovetail with one another, but also illuminated a corner of first-century history as a whole. His article factors into the approach of this book; his insight has exercised an influence on me more broadly.

Professor Crook's patience in conversation carried on even as I shifted my focus to the Aramaic environment of earliest Christianity: although that line of inquiry has been my more pressing concern in the intervening years, his insight also remained in my mind. For differing reasons, with interests that did not entirely coincide, and at very different stages of scholarship, he and I shared the conviction that, despite the claims of some fashions in interpretation, no body of literature can be adequately understood when it is taken in isolation. Historical environment is always and everywhere a key to meaning, no matter what the text studied. My engagement with Berenice and her family matured only after Professor Crook's death, but his influence has been palpable.

Another classicist, James Romm, issued the invitation for me to write on Berenice, whom I had recommended to him as the most interesting and least appreciated member of the Herodian dynasty. Yale's Ancient Lives series has proven to be the ideal setting, since recent scholarship has prepared the way to focus on particular Herodians within their contexts. Yet two challenges remained. Berenice herself was effaced and distorted in virtually all the sources, and those sources themselves are not familiar to most readers. My hope is that this work – completed during consultation with James Romm and Yale University Press editors Heather Gold, Elizabeth Sylvia, Chelsea Connelly, Susan Laity, and Beth Lindop, as well as copyeditor Julie Carlson, proofreader Dan Heaton, and indexer Emma Warnken Johnson – assesses Berenice in history such that her intents come to the surface. Readers are also provided with the coordinates of the sources concerned, so that they can evaluate the analysis, and appreciate Berenice's unparalleled trajectory without the obstruction of unnecessary digressions. My intention is to offer both an illustration of how to infer a life from history as well as a substantial engagement with Berenice herself, a person it has become my privilege to know.

Index

Agrippa (son of Drusilla), 68, 126–127, 172–173n45

Agrippa, Marcus Vipsanius, 41–42, 45

Agrippa I (father of Berenice): children of, 4, 13, 24–26, 46–48, 71, 73, 75–76, 160n18; death of, 52–56, 60, 65, 142, 150, 163–164n5; genealogy of, 153; namesake of, 41–42, 45; and Nazirite practice, 80–81, 86, 166n29; and Roman imperial favor, 17–18, 20–24, 30, 37–40, 63, 144, 150, 162n17; and the Temple in Jerusalem, 29, 31–36, 41–45, 51–52, 95

Agrippa II (brother of Berenice): alleged incest with Berenice, 2, 5, 46, 76–79, 110, 123, 131–132, 138–139, 148, 172n38; in Caesarea Philippi, 63–67, 151; death of, 121, 143, 152; early life in Rome, 46–47, 54–56, 58–59, 61–62; and the Flavian dynasty, 111–115, 122, 124, 132, 151–152; genealogy of, 153; during the Jewish War, 100–107, 109–111, 121, 169n27; meeting with Paul, 82, 85–86, 151; and Nazirite practice, 80–81, 86; and sister's marriages, 68, 71, 75–77; and the Temple in Jerusalem, 61–63, 80, 91–97, 99

Agrippina (wife of Claudius), 62, 67

Agrippinus (son of Mariamme), 71

Albinus, Lucceius (procurator of Judea), 94–97, 151

Alexander (son of Herod the Great), 15–16, 67, 143, 149, 153

Alexander, Marcus Julius (husband of Berenice): and Agrippa I, 39, 140; betrothal to Berenice, 11–12, 23–26, 64, 71; death of, 47, 142, 163n29; marriage to Berenice, 29, 48, 75, 150, 153, 160–161n18

Alexander, Tiberius Julius (procurator of Judea), 59, 61, 69, 91, 100, 102, 115–116, 118, 140, 151

Alexander the Alabarch: and Agrippa I, 21–22, 25, 30, 36, 39, 41; and Judaism, 59; and son's marriage to Berenice, 11, 23–24; and the Temple in Jerusalem, 29, 32, 39

Alexander the Great, 12

Alexandria, Egypt: Agrippa I in, 23–25, 30, 41; and Agrippa II, 100; Berenice in, 11, 13, 29–30, 39, 64; and Caligula, 35; Cyprus in, 21, 39; Jewish community in, 11–13, 31–32, 102, 155; and Judea, 94–95, 104; Mariamme in, 71; Vespasian in, 115–116

Ananias (high priest), 61, 84, 91, 96

Ananus (high priest), 94–96

Andrew (apostle), 63

Antioch, 20, 103–104, 150

Antiochus (king of Commagene), 68, 73; as character in *Bérénice*, 134–137

Antipas (son of Herod the Great): and Agrippa I, 20–21, 30; and Christianity, 18, 58, 73, 85–86, 150; exile of, 30, 150; as founder of Tiberias, 19–20, 150; genealogy of, 153; marriage to Herodias, 18, 67, 160n8; as tetrarch, 16, 23, 37, 63–64, 144, 149

Index

Antipater (father of Herod the Great), 13, 143–144, 149, 153
Antipater (son of Herod the Great), 149
anti-Semitism, 3, 31
Antonia (daughter of Mark Antony), 21, 23, 30, 36, 67
Antonia Fortress, Jerusalem, 56, 58, 84, 100, 102, 118
Antony, Mark, 2, 13, 21, 84, 149, 172n38; and Cleopatra, 35, 75, 159–160n5
Apion, 31–32
apostles. See *individual apostles*
Archelaus (son of Helcias), 71
Archelaus (son of Herod the Great): as ethnarch, 16, 23, 37, 64, 144; genealogy of, 153; marriage to Glaphyra, 67; removal from power, 38, 54, 149
Areopagus, Athens, 4, 96, 151, 168n13
Aristobulus (son of Herod of Chalcis), 48, 56, 61, 63, 65, 143
Aristobulus (son of Herod the Great; grandfather of Berenice), 15–16, 48, 149, 153, 160n6
Armenia, 143
Augustus (Roman emperor): accession of, 149; family of, 21, 41, 113; and Herod's sons, 16, 32, 37–38, 54, 63, 95; and Herod the Great, 13, 15; and Judaism, 42
Azizus (king of Emesa), 68, 77, 151

Babylonian Empire, 15, 124
baptism, 73, 82
Bar Kokhba (Simon bar Kosibah), 145
Beirut, 51–52, 96–97
Berenice (children). *See* Berenicianus; Hycranus (son of Berenice)
Berenice (daughter of Mariamme), 71
Berenice (faith). *See* Judaism; Nazirites
Berenice (family), 153. *See also* Agrippa I; Agrippa II; Cyprus; Drusilla; Mariamme
Berenice (life dates): birth, 11, 18–19, 25; death, 121, 143, 148; timeline of, 149–151
Berenice (meaning of name), 1
Berenice (modern portrayals of), 132–138, 173–174n12, 174n23
Berenice (myths and conspiracies about), 138, 174n28, 175n30
Bérénice (Racine play). *See* Racine, Jean
Berenice (relationships). *See* Alexander, Marcus Julius; Herod of Chalcis; Polemon; Titus
Berenice (sources on), 155–157. *See also* Dio Cassius; Josephus; Juvenal; Quintilian; Suetonius
Berenice (statues and inscriptions of), 4, 39, 45, 53, 96, 141, 151, 168n6
Berenicianus (son of Berenice), 60–61, 65, 74, 76, 143, 153
Bethsaida (town), 63
Bible: Acts, 43–44, 52–53, 56, 69, 72, 83–87, 156, 167n32, 168n6; Corinthians, 44; Esther, 34; Haggai, 15; John, 63; Luke, 58, 85, 167n32; Mark, 160n8; Matthew, 37, 160n8; New Testament, 38, 138, 169n27; Revelation, 129–130; Romans, 42, 82–83; Samuel, 15; Zechariah, 15. *See also* Torah
biography (genre), 46–47, 138
bios (a life), 7, 47, 139
Bouquet, Carole, 135, 157, 174n23
Britain (Roman province), 46, 104, 148
Brown, Dan: *Da Vinci Code, The,* 137
Brutus, Marcus Junius, 149

Caecina Alienus, Aulus, 125
Caesar, Julius, 42, 113, 137, 149
Caesar, Sextus (governor of Syria), 149
Caesarea Maritima (city), 39, 45, 52–53, 84–86, 98, 100, 112, 119, 164n7
Caesarea Philippi (city): Agrippa I in,

Index

30, 39, 41; Agrippa II in, 62–63, 65, 67, 96, 100, 132, 143, 151; Berenice in, 63, 65, 67, 75–77, 79, 122, 132, 139, 143, 151; Berenice's childhood in, 24–26; Philip in, 63–64, 144; renaming to Neronias, 100; Titus in, 106, 109, 119–121, 127, 151
Caiaphas (high priest), 58
Caligula (Roman emperor): and Agrippa I, 23, 29–31, 38–39, 41, 51, 64, 122, 150; and Alexandria, 12; death of, 36, 150; early life of, 21–23; and the Temple in Jerusalem, 29, 32–36, 150
Cassius Longinus, Gaius, 149
"cattishness," 46, 110, 138
Chaera, Cassius (tribune), 36
Chalcis, 40, 47, 52, 60–64, 68, 150. *See also* Herod of Chalcis
Chepey, Stuart, 166n29, 167n31–32, 168n7, 169n24
Chilton, Bruce, 155
Christianity: and Agrippa II, 85; and Berenice conspiracy theories, 138; Herodian dynasty in, 37, 53, 162n13; and Julian, 145–147; and the Nazirites, 81–83, 168n7; persecution of, 98, 129–130, 143, 151; use of term, 44, 150. *See also* baptism; Bible; Jesus of Nazareth; *individual apostles*
Cilicia, 74–76, 151
circumcision, 12, 68–74, 77–78, 82, 140–141, 165n9
Claudius (Roman emperor): and Agrippa I, 36–40, 51–52; and Agrippa II, 54–55, 58, 61–65, 150; and Christianity, 43, 85–86; death of, 67, 151; and Herod of Chalcis, 55, 60; lineage, 21
Cleopatra (queen of Egypt): accession of, 149; comparison to Berenice, 2, 4, 25, 130, 137, 172n38, 172n42; and Mark Antony, 35, 75, 159–160n5
Cleopatra (wife of Gessius Florus), 98
Cleopatra (wife of Herod the Great), 16
coins: of Agrippa I, 40, 162n17; of Cyprus, 26; of Felix, 69; of Herod of Chalcis, 40; of *Judaea Capta,* 122; of Philip, 63–64, 165n27; of Polemon, 75, 79, 166n22
Colchis, 74–76, 151
Collingwood, Robin, 46, 110, 138–139, 142–143, 175n31. *See also* "cattishness"
Commagene, 68, 73, 137
consilium (Roman council), 121–122
Constantine (Roman emperor), 145–146, 157
Corinth, 19
Corneille, Pierre: *Tite et Bérénice,* 133–134, 137, 174n25
Costabarus (husband of Salome), 69–70
Crispina, Julia (possible daughter of Berenicianus), 143
crucifixion, 37, 58, 85, 94, 99, 150
Crusades, 145
Cumanus, Ventidius (procurator in Judea), 61–62, 65, 151, 156
Cutiliae, 126–127
Cydnus River, 75
Cynics, 77, 123–125, 130, 139
Cyprus (mother of Berenice), 13, 17–18, 20–22, 25–26, 39, 150, 153, 160n18
Cyrus (Persian emperor), 124

Damascus, 19
Demetrius (alabarch of Alexandria), 71
Dinah (biblical figure), 70
Dio Cassius: on Agrippa I, 40; as ancient source, 156; on Berenice, 3, 122, 127, 130, 140, 148; on Messalina, 131; *Roman History,* 155; on the Temple of Peace, 120; on Vespasian, 117, 123

Index

Diogenes (Cynic critic of the Flavians), 123
divorce (in the ancient world), 26, 68–72, 78, 140–141, 151
Domitian (Roman emperor): and Berenice, 144; and founding of Flavian dynasty, 109, 113, 116–117, 120, 122; Juvenal on, 3; reign of, 129–131, 145, 152, 173n3
Drusilla (sister of Berenice): death of, 125–126, 173n45; early life of, 17, 45, 53; genealogy of, 153; marriage to Azizus, 68, 70, 74, 151; marriage to Felix, 68–69, 73–74, 76–77, 91, 110, 141, 151; and Paul's visit to Jerusalem, 84, 86; relationship with Berenice, 75, 77, 110, 131
Drusus (son of Agrippa I), 17, 153
Drusus (son of Tiberius), 17, 150

Egypt: Judaism in, 19, 102; name of Berenice in, 1, 30, 175n30; religion of, 99; and Roman coups, 115–116; wealth of, 75–76, 100, 117, 140. *See also* Alexandria
Eleazar (son of Ananias), 102
Emesa, 68, 79, 151
Emmerich, Roland: *Those About to Die*, 137–138
emperors of Rome. See *individual emperors*
Epiphanes (son of Antiochus), 68, 73
Epitome de Caesaribus, 125, 172n41
Esau (brother of Jacob), 74
Essenes (Jewish movement), 80
Euphrates River, 116
Eusebius, 157, 168n6
Evans, Katherine, 163n29

Fadus, Cuspius (procurator of Judea), 55–56, 58–60, 150
Felix, Antonius (procurator of Judea): marriage to Drusilla, 68–69, 73–74, 76–77, 91, 110, 141, 151; and Paul's visit to Jerusalem, 84–86; as procurator of Judea, 62, 65, 79–80, 151
Festus, Porcius (procurator of Judea), 85–86, 91–94, 121, 151, 168n6
Flaccus, Lucius Pomponius (legate of Rome), 20
Flavian dynasty. *See* Domitian; Titus; Vespasian
Flavius Josephus. *See* Josephus
Florus, Gessius (procurator of Judea), 97–103, 131, 141, 151
Freeman, Philip, 147

Gaius (son of Germanicus). *See* Caligula (Roman emperor)
Galba (Roman emperor), 107, 111–113, 116, 151
Galilee: and Agrippa I, 21, 30, 38–39; and Antipas, 16, 18, 73; governance of, 64; during the Jewish War, 103, 105–107, 109, 113, 122, 131; and the Temple in Jerusalem, 19, 61; violence in, 66
Gallus, Gaius Cestius (legate in Syria), 100, 103, 151
Gambetti, Sandra: *Alexandrian Riots of 38 C.E. and the Persecution of the Jews, The*, 155
Gamla, 106
Gaul (Roman province), 30, 107, 111
Gaulanitis, 16, 23, 30, 38–39, 64, 66, 122, 150
Germania (Roman provinces), 111, 113
Germanicus (adopted son of Tiberius), 22
gladiatorial games, 52, 119, 141, 141
Glaphyra (wife of Archelaus), 67
Goodman, Martin, 14, 155, 159n5, 162n13
Greece, 104. *See also* Areopagus, Athens

Index

Hegesippus, 157, 169n24
Helena (queen of Adiabene), 80, 166n29
Heras (Cynic critic of the Flavians), 123
Herodian dynasty (genealogy of), 153. *See also* Agrippa I; Agrippa II; Berenice; Herod the Great; *other individual family members*
Herodian palace, Jerusalem, 92, 99, 101–103
Herodias (daughter of Aristobulus), 18, 21, 30, 67–68, 160n8
Herod of Chalcis (brother of Agrippa I): death of, 60–61, 142, 151; lineage of, 40, 150; marriage to Berenice, 47–48, 55, 75–76, 140, 150, 153; and the Temple in Jerusalem, 56–60, 91, 151
Herod the Great (king of Judea): and the Antonia fortress, 84; and Caesarea Maritima, 39, 52; in Christianity, 37, 53, 162n13; genealogy of, 153; reign of, 2, 13–15, 70–71, 149, 160n5, 164n5; sources on, 5, 162n23; successors of, 23–24, 30, 38, 51, 54, 62–66, 94, 125, 143–144; and the Temple in Jerusalem, 32, 40–42, 92, 97, 124
Hispania (Roman province), 107, 111
homosexuality (in the ancient world), 46, 126, 130
Hyrcanus (ethnarch of Judea), 149
Hyrcanus (son of Berenice), 60–61, 65, 74, 76, 143, 153

Idumea, 14–17, 20–21, 41, 60, 118, 137
Ilan, Tal, 25, 115, 160n18, 161n19
incest (alleged between Berenice and Agrippa II), 2, 5, 46, 76–79, 110, 123, 131–132, 138–139, 148, 172n38
Ishmael ben Phabi, 91–93
Islam, 145

Jacob (biblical figure), 70, 74
James (apostle, son of Zebedee), 43–44, 53, 85, 167n32
James (brother of Jesus), 83, 94–96, 151, 157, 168n6, 169n24
Jerusalem: Agrippa II in, 101–102, 169n27; Berenice in, 75–76, 79, 81, 92, 97–100, 169n24, 169n27; and Herod the Great, 64, 71, 144; Jewish community in, 42, 44, 72; during the Jewish War, 102–103, 106–107, 111–112, 116–120, 127, 151; Paul's visit to, 69, 81–86, 91, 94–95, 121, 151, 156, 168n6; relationship with Rome, 15, 32, 35, 38, 57–58, 130–131, 150; resistance and protests in, 42, 52, 61, 79–80, 91; taxes in, 36. *See also* Antonia Fortress; Herodian palace; Temple in Jerusalem
Jesus (son of Damneus), 96
Jesus (son of Gamaliel), 97
Jesus of Nazareth: birth of, 37; crucifixion of, 37, 58, 85–86, 94, 150; early followers of, 43–44, 63, 72–73, 82–83, 150; and the Trinity, 145–146
Jewish revolt (132–135 CE), 145–146
Jewish War (66–74 CE): aftermath of, 121–122, 127, 145–146; beginnings of, 98–102, 131, 141, 169n27; capture of Jerusalem during, 1, 117–120, 124, 151; early battles in, 102–107, 109; founding of Flavian dynasty during, 110–117; Roman victory in, 120, 170n38; sources on, 157
John the Baptist, 18, 67, 85–86, 150, 160n8
Jonathan (high priest), 79
Jordan, Ruth, 160n18, 172n38
Jordan River, 16, 54, 56, 160n5
Josephus (as ancient source), 155–157; on Agrippa I, 22, 25–26, 33–34, 43–44, 52–53, 162n17; on Agrippa II, 54,

Josephus (as ancient source) (*continued*) 92, 115, 169n27; on Agrippina, 67; on Ananus, 95; on Antipas, 18–19; on Berenice, 5–6, 53, 74–76, 87, 110, 121, 123, 131–132, 141; on Berenice and Agrippa II, 76–77, 101, 131, 138–139, 148; on Berenice and Polemon, 74–79; on circumcision, 70–72; on Cuspius Fadus, 55–56, 60; on Cyprus, 21; on divorce, 69, 140; on Drusilla and Felix, 68–69; on the Herodian dynasty, 143; on Nazirite practice, 80, 166n29; on Poppaea Sabina, 93, 98; on Rome, 42, 162n23; on the Temple in Jerusalem, 45, 79–80, 97, 124, 131, 145; on Tiberius Julius Alexander, 59, 102, 116; on Titus, 109, 112, 117–119, 141; on Vespasian, 112–115, 117, 120

Josephus (life): birth of, 150; meeting with Poppaea Sabina, 98; role in Jewish War, 103, 105–106, 117–118, 170n38

Josephus (works), 155–157; *Jewish Antiquities,* 95, 110, 121, 131, 151, 171n35; *Jewish War,* 95, 103, 109, 114, 120, 123–124, 131, 145, 152; *Life,* 110, 121, 131–132, 152

Jotapata, 105, 114, 170n38

Judaism: and Agrippa I, 33, 43–44; in Alexandria, 11–13, 31–32, 102, 155; and Berenice, 1, 3–4, 78, 97–99, 139–140, 147–148; in Caesarea Philippi, 63; and Caligula, 29, 31; circumcision in, 71–72, 74; divorce in, 69–70; and Emesa, 68; and Herod the Great, 14; in Jerusalem, 42, 44, 72, 80–81; and Polemon, 79; and Poppaea, 93, 98; and power, 164n15; Rabbinic, 14, 20, 45, 69, 141, 147, 161n19, 167n32; Roman relationship with, 35–36, 40, 42, 56–57, 93, 102–103, 141–147, 162n23; Second Temple, 19–20, 40, 69–70, 142, 161n19; and Tiberius Julius Alexander, 59; and Titus, 5. *See also* Bible; Essenes; Mishnah; Nazirites; Pharisees; synagogues; Talmud; Torah

Judas the Galilean, 59, 149

Judea: Agrippa I as ruler of, 20, 30, 34, 37–39, 41, 45, 51, 55; Archelaus as ruler of, 16; Berenice in, 1, 121–122, 140, 145; Christianity in, 44, 73; Herodian influence in, 11, 58, 66, 127, 130, 143; Herod the Great as ruler of, 2, 13–16; during the Jewish War, 5, 98, 102, 104, 106–107, 109–117; Judaism in, 19, 36, 72; revolts and resistance in, 2, 35, 54, 65, 67, 86; Roman administration of, 58, 61, 64, 69, 76, 93–95, 149–151. *See also* Jerusalem; Yavneh

Julian (Roman emperor), 145–147

Julio-Claudian dynasty. *See* Augustus; Caligula; Claudius; Nero; Tiberius

Justus of Tiberias, 121, 131, 171n35

Juvenal: sixth satire, 2–4, 6, 46, 76, 132, 137–139, 148, 155

Kabi, Joseph (high priest), 94

Kokkinos, Nikos, 155

Kreuzpaintner, Marco: *Those About to Die*, 137–138

Kropp, Andreas, 162n17

legates. See *individual legates*

Le Moyne, Pierre, 133

Levin, Daniel: *Last Ember, The,* 137

Lusitania (Roman provinces), 111

Lysias, Claudius (Roman tribune), 84–85

Maccabees (first book of), 57

Maccabees: and circumcision, 73;

Index

Herodian connections to, 13–17, 41, 45, 60–61, 142, 149; and Jerusalem, 57, 92
Macrobius, 160n6
Macurdy, Grace Harriet, 132, 155, 168n13
Malatha, 17–18
Malthake (wife of Herod the Great), 16, 149, 153
Mamaea, Julia (wife of Polemon), 75, 79, 166n22
Marcus Julius Alexander. *See* Alexander, Marcus Julius
Mariamme (sister of Berenice), 17, 20, 25, 45, 53, 71, 75–76, 153
Mariamme I (wife of Herod the Great), 15–16, 45, 61, 143–144, 149, 153, 159n5
marriage (in the ancient world), 18, 24–27, 67–77, 140, 165n9. *See also* circumcision; divorce
Marsus, Gaius Vibius (legate in Syria), 51–53, 56
Masada, 151, 170n38
Mason, Steve: *History of the Jewish War*, 155, 157
Mediterranean Sea, 35, 39, 75
Messalina (wife of Claudius), 131
Mishnah, 19–20, 45, 80, 167n32; Nazir, 166n29; Yoma, 99
Mommsen, Theodor, 2
Moses, 12, 72
Mount Vesuvius, 126–127, 148
Mucianus, Gaius Licinius (legate of Syria), 112, 114, 116, 170n7

Nazianzus, Gregory, 146
Nazirites (Jewish ritual practitioners): and Agrippa I, 43, 81; and Berenice, 81, 86, 97–99, 141, 151, 169n24; and James (brother of Jesus), 94–95, 151, 168n7; and Paul, 81, 83, 91, 167n31; vow of, 43, 80, 166n29, 167n32
Neoplatonism, 146–147
Nero (Roman emperor): accession of, 67, 151; ancestry of, 21; comparison with Titus, 126, 130, 139; death of, 107, 111, 151; and Herod of Chalcis, 143; and Judea, 92–94, 104; persecution of Christians by, 98, 151; and Polemon, 74, 79; and Poppaea Sabina, 93, 97–98
Neronias (city). *See* Caesarea Philippi (city)
Nerva (Roman emperor), 131, 138
Nicholas of Damascus, 5
numismatics. *See* coins

Octavia (sister of Augustus), 21
Octavian. *See* Augustus (Roman emperor)
ostraca, 47, 163n29
Otho (Roman emperor), 111–112, 116, 151

Pallas (brother of Felix), 62, 80
Panias (city). *See* Caesarea Philippi (city)
Parthian Empire, 13–14, 32, 144, 149
Paul (apostle): birthplace of, 75; conversion of, 150; in Corinthians, 44; Letter to the Galatians, 73, 82; Letter to the Romans, 42, 82, 151; and Nazarite practice, 81–83, 91, 94, 167n31–32, 168n6; visit to Jerusalem, 69, 81–86, 91, 95, 121, 151, 156
Pentateuch. *See* Torah
Perea, 16, 38, 54, 64, 66
Persian Empire, 124
Peter (apostle), 53, 63, 72
Petronius, Publius (legate in Syria), 32–36, 51
Pharisees (Jewish movement), 80
Philadelphia, 54
Philip (son of Herod the Great), 16, 23–25, 30, 37, 63–64, 144, 149–150, 153, 165n27

Index

Philippi (city), 149
philo-Judaism, 42, 129
Philo of Alexandria: and Agrippa I, 24–25, 33–36, 39; death of, 72–73, 156; *Embassy to Gaius*, 36, 155; philosophy of, 12–13, 72; on protests in Alexandria, 24, 31–32; relationship to Berenice, 24, 29
philo-Romanism, 42, 147
Phoenicia, 51
Photius: *Bibliotheke*, 53, 156, 164n7
Pilate, Pontius, 37, 58, 73, 85, 99, 150
Piso, Gaius Calpernius, 111
Plato, 12, 34, 72
Plutarch, 107, 157
Polemon (king of Pontus, Colchis, and Cilicia; husband of Berenice), 74–79, 110, 140, 151, 153, 166n22
Pompeii, 126–127
Pompey, 15, 57
Pontus, 74–76, 151
Poppaea Sabina (wife of Nero), 93, 97–98, 104, 111
Praetorian Guard, 36–37, 58, 123, 125, 150
priesthood (in Jerusalem), 42, 56–59, 79–80, 85–86, 91–98, 102, 118. See also *individual high priests*
Primus, Antonius (Roman general), 116
Priscus, Helvidius, 123
procurators of Judea. See *individual procurators*
protests and riots (challenging Roman rule): against Agrippa I in Alexandria, 24; against Caligula's statue, 31–33, 36; against Cuspius Fadus, 56; against Felix, 65; against Gessius Florus, 99–101; against James's execution, 95–96; against Paul's visit to the Temple, 83–84; against Pontius Pilate, 99; against Quirinius's taxes, 59; against Ventidius Cumanus, 61. *See also* Jewish War

Quadratus, Ummidius (legate of Syria), 61–62
Quintilian, 3, 121–122, 148, 155
Quirinius, Publius Sulpicius (legate to Syria), 59, 150

Racine, Jean: *Bérénice*, 125, 133–138, 157, 173–174n12, 174n23
resistance to Roman rule. *See* Jewish revolt; Jewish War; protests and riots (against Roman rule)
Roddaz, Jean-Michel, 42
Roman Empire. *See* Rome (city); *individual provinces*
Roman Republic, 113
Rome (city): Agrippa I in, 16–17, 20–24, 31, 33, 35–36, 39; Agrippa II in, 46–47, 54–56, 58–59, 61–62, 64–65, 111–112, 152; and Alexandria, 11–12; Berenice in, 2–3, 78, 121–122, 124–126, 131–132, 139–140, 142, 152, 172n42; Christians in, 82, 85–86, 98, 147, 161, 168n6; Colosseum, 127, 129, 148; fires in, 127, 148, 151; founding of Flavian dynasty in, 106, 111–117; Herod's sons in, 15–16, 30, 149; Ishmael ben Phabi's embassy to, 92–93; Jewish community in, 40, 42; and Judea, 13–15; in modern literature, 133–137; Philo of Alexandria in, 24, 32; Temple of Peace, 120, 122, 124, 145, 151; triumphs in, 119–120, 123, 151
Rosenblum, Jordan D., 160n6

Sabinus, Titus Flavius (brother of Vespasian), 115
Sadducees, 94–95, 149
Salome (daughter of Herodias), 18, 160n8
Salome (sister of Herod the Great), 26, 69–71

Index

Samaria: Herodian rule of, 16, 37–38, 59, 122, 149; Roman rule of, 54–55, 58, 64; violence in, 58, 61, 65–66
Sassanian Empire, 145
Schalit, Abraham, 162n17
Schwartz, Daniel R., 155–156
Scudéry, Madeleine de, 132–133, 137
Second Sophistic, 156
Second Temple. *See* Temple in Jerusalem
Second Triumvirate, 149
Segrais, Jean Regnault, 133
Sejanus (Roman prefect), 58, 150
Sepphoris, 105
Septuagint, 12, 155, 170n38. *See also* Judaism
sexuality. *See* homosexuality (in the ancient world); incest (alleged between Berenice and Agrippa II)
Shechem (biblical figure), 70
sicarii, 79–80, 86, 91, 96, 118
Simon (apostle). *See* Peter (apostle)
Simon (Jerusalem teacher in debate with Agrippa I), 44
Slaughter of the Innocents, 37, 162n13
Smallwood, E. Mary, 125, 172n42
Solomon's Temple, 124
sources (ancient), 155–157. *See also* coins; ostraca; statues; *individual primary sources*
Sporus (slave of Nero), 104
statues: of Berenice, 4, 39, 45, 53, 96, 141, 151, 168n13; of Roman emperors, 24, 31–35, 39, 51, 150
Suetonius: as ancient source, 156–157; on Berenice and Titus, 125–126, 130, 140, 148, 172n42; on Caligula, 36; on Claudius, 67; on Domitian, 129–130; on Nero, 98, 104
Syllaeus (Nabatean suitor of Herod's sister), 70
synagogues, 24, 31, 51, 72, 98. *See also* Temple in Jerusalem
Syria (Roman province): and Agrippa I, 21, 39; in *Bérénice,* 135; and Drusilla, 69; governors of, 20, 149; and Judea, 85, 95, 100, 103; legates of, 32, 51, 58, 61, 112, 114, 150–151; violence in, 102

Tacitus: as ancient source, 156–157; on Aristobulus, 143; on Berenice, 112, 115, 130, 148; on Caligula, 32, 34; on Felix, 68, 79; on the Flavian dynasty, 105; on Judea, 61; on Titus, 112, 130; on the Year of the Four Emperors, 111–113
Talmud, 20
Tarsus (city), 42, 75, 84, 121
Temple in Jerusalem: and Agrippa I, 35–36, 40–45, 51; and Agrippa II, 61–63, 66, 81, 86, 91–92; and Ananus, 95; and Berenice, 1, 55, 66, 81, 91, 101, 141–143, 148; and Berenice's Nazirite vow, 86, 97, 99; Caligula's statue in, 29, 31–34, 150; destruction of (70 CE), 1, 5, 78, 118–120, 124, 151, 161n19; First Temple, 12; and Herod the Chalcis, 60; during the Jewish War, 100–102; Nazirite practice in, 80–83, 86, 94, 167n31; possible restoration of, 2, 124, 126–127, 130–131, 141, 145–147; role in Judaism, 19, 69, 80; Roman intervention at, 56–59, 61, 84, 93; and the sicarii, 79–80. *See also* Antonia Fortress; Herodian palace
Tertullus (attorney), 84
tetrarchs. *See* Antipas (son of Herod the Great); Philip (son of Herod the Great)
Theudas, 55–56, 150
Those About to Die (television series), 137–138

Index

Tiberias (city): Agrippa I in, 18–20, 25, 30, 32, 35, 39, 52, 150; Berenice in, 18–20, 64; Herodian loss of, 103, 105–106, 121
Tiberius (Roman emperor), 17–19, 21–23, 31–32, 113, 150
Tiberius Gemellus (son of Tiberius), 22–23
Titus (Roman emperor): accession of, 2, 126, 152, 170n7; death of, 3, 127, 129, 148, 152; and founding of Flavian dynasty, 112–115; during the Jewish War, 1, 104–107, 109–111, 116–120, 124, 151; Josephus on, 5, 105, 110, 131; and legate to Judea, 143; relationship with Berenice, 2–3, 106, 109, 115, 120–126, 139–142, 145, 151, 153, 172n42; in seventeenth-century literature, 132–137; Suetonius on, 130, 148
Torah, 12, 18–20, 45, 82, 145; Deuteronomy, 45; Exodus, 12; Genesis, 70; Leviticus, 160n8; Numbers, 43, 145, 167n32. *See also* Bible
Trajan (Roman emperor), 131
triumphs, 119–120, 122–123, 151
Vergil: *Aeneid,* 125, 172n41
Vespasian (Roman emperor): critics of, 123, 125; death of, 126, 137, 152; and Judean legates, 143; military campaign in Judea, 104–107, 109–111, 122; relationship to Berenice, 120–121, 133, 140; rise to emperor, 112–117, 119, 151
Vitellius, Aulus (Roman emperor), 111–113, 115–116, 151
Vitellius, Lucius (legate in Syria), 32, 58

Wasserstein, Abraham and David: *Legend of the Septuagint,* 155
Wilde, Oscar: *Salome,* 18
Wilker, Julia, 155
women (in ancient sources), 25–26, 131–132

Yavneh, Judea, 31, 100–101
Year of the Four Emperors, 107, 111–114, 116
Yosef bar Mattityahu. *See* Josephus

Zerubbabel, 15